Decades of Differences
Making It Work

Bonnie Hagemann
Ken Gronbach
with Foreword by Jim Bolt

Published by: HRD Press, Inc.
22 Amherst Road
Amherst, MA 01002
413-253-3488
800-822-2801 (U.S. and Canada)
413-253-3490 (fax)
www.hrdpress.com

ISBN 978-1-59996-213-9

Editorial services by Sally Farnham
Production services by Jean Miller
Cover design by Eileen Klockars

Dedicated to Todd and Linda
whose loving support and sacrifice of time
made this book possible

Contents

About the Author

 **Bonnie Hagemann** is the CEO of Executive Development Associates, a 28-year-old internationally known boutique consulting firm in custom executive development. In addition to leading the firm, Hagemann has a unique background and expertise in developing leaders. She specializes in executive development, executive coaching, and high potential development.

To date, Hagemann has conducted coaching programs for over 65 leaders in medium and large organizations including seven organizational presidents. She has delivered over 250 presentations and speeches on leadership, team building, communication, conflict, and behavior. She has 11 published works, is often quoted as a subject matter expert in the press, and has a book under contract to be released in 2010 on the shifting workforce demographics and their impact on leadership.

Contact: bhagemann@executivedevelopment.com
www.executivedevelopment.com
1-866-EXECDEV, ext. 201.

About the Author

Ken Gronbach is an expert demographer, futurist, and generational marketer. He is the author of *The Age Curve, Common Census,* and numerous published articles. As current CEO of KGC Direct, Ken is internationally recognized for his uniquely accurate theories and his capability for predicting and forecasting marketing and societal phenomena.

Gronbach is a seasoned marketing professional and dynamic public speaker who led KGA Advertising for 21 years, growing it to a $40 million, 40-person marketing, advertising, and merchandising machine by anticipating markets and growing clients. Ken's ability to forecast the future of commerce, culture, and economics is unparalleled in his field. Long-range planning without Ken's insights are like driving at night without lights.

Contact: ken@kgcdirect.com
www.kgcdirect. com
1-860-345-4604

Foreword

I am delighted to introduce you to this exciting book on the dramatic shifting demographics as well as the sledgehammer impact being felt in the workplace, including by leaders and those being led. This important book clearly describes that impact and the implications, both for today and the future.

My life's work has been helping global 500 organizations ensure that they have the executive and leadership talent needed to achieve their strategic objectives. I've always worked with CEOs and other senior executives to create executive development strategies, systems, and programs that develop the capabilities they need to achieve their vision and execute their strategies.

Part of my consulting process includes ensuring that clients are aware of key global forces and trends so that they are not caught off guard by critical challenges that could impact the ability to successfully implement their strategy.

Decades of Differences covers one of those challenges that every leader in every organization needs to be aware of. I believe this topic is critical today, especially because of the impact that generational differences are having in the workplace and on our leadership development efforts. And perhaps it will be even more important over the next 10 years for the development of the next generation of leaders.

There has been a lot said about generational differences: perhaps too much heat and not enough light for many of us. Hagemann and Gronbach have addressed the topic so that we can actually understand what this means in a practical and meaningful way, and, more importantly, know what to do about it—whether you are a top-level executive, a current leader, an aspiring leader, or someone being led.

While the workplace is always shifting, we seem to be feeling the changes now more like the rumblings of an approaching earthquake more than the gentle adjustments of the past. With the technology revolution, change is coming much faster, and the younger generations just might be in the driver's seat this time around.

Each of us has our own idea about what these diverse generations, technology, and globalization are going to mean, but tying Hagemann's years of leadership development and talent management experience with Gronbach's expertise in demographics provides a fresh and highly relevant look into these changes including the associated opportunities, problems, and possible solutions. By the way, as you turn the pages, you'll notice the authors poke a little fun at each of the generations, which makes the book quite enjoyable.

The authors have done a good job of combining research and experience to explain how shifting demographics are forever changing the workplace and leadership as we know it. It is definitely worth your time to sit down with your favorite latte, coffee, tea, or adult beverage to explore the richness of our diversity through the lens of the generations.

James F. Bolt
Founder, Bolt Consulting
Cofounder, FrED

Selected by *Financial Times* as one of the leading experts in executive/leadership development, *Harvard Business Review* author, author of three books including *Strategic Executive Development* and *The Future of Executive Development*, *Fast Company* magazine online columnist, named by Linkage, Inc. as one of the top 50 executive coaches in the world, editor of *The 2007 Pfeiffer Annual: Leadership Development*.

Acknowledgments

John Maketa, our mutual friend and colleague. Without John's masterful networking and timely introduction, this book would never have happened.

Robert Carkhuff and Mark Snow, our HRD Press publishers. Their intelligent insight, laid-back style, and sensible guidance made every part of the writing process enjoyable and stress free.

Sally Farnham, our HRD Press editor. Sally's editorial expertise and guidance made this collection of insights into a cohesive work.

Dawn Ciarlone, EDA's Director of Operations. Dawn's operational support and personal encouragement during the writing process gave us boosts of energy at just the right times.

Our collective clients and friends who allow us to be a part of their lives whether for a short period of time or over a lifetime. Their openness to share gave us interesting stories and insights that we have been able to share with you, the reader.

Our children—Libby and Hayle (Ken and Linda's children), and Erin and Joel (Todd and Bonnie's children)—who inspire us to use our talents and try to help others when and where we can.

To you, the reader, for sharing your valuable time and reading *Decades of Differences.* It is our wish that you will find at least one thing in this book that will truly help you as you lead and learn with these diverse generations.

Introduction

At about 6:00 p.m. while wrapping up a Monday evening coaching call, Hagemann asks her client to participate in our survey on the shifting demographics in the workplace. The response, one that we have grown accustomed to, is that of exuberance. This chief nursing officer in a large healthcare network in Florida excitedly jumps into a story about a nurse manager who has been asked by some of her Gen Y employees to "meet with their parents." That's right: instead of a parent/teacher conference, it's a parent/manager conference. Are you shocked? Well, that's just the beginning of the new world order in the workplace. The changes going on in today's work environment are shocking, funny, and even a little scary from time to time. But, one thing is for sure: the changes are not boring. So we think you are going to enjoy our journey into both the macro and the micro theater of today's workplace with features including the massive shift in the demographics, the technology revolution, and so much more. We have a lot to tell you and hopefully a little guidance and comfort to offer along the way, so we better get started.

Let's begin with a foundation...

We now have three primary generations in the United States' workforce. This workforce is currently estimated at approximately 140 million between the ages of 20 to 60.

1. The massive Generation Y (born between 1985 and 2004)

2. The small Generation X (born between 1965 and 1984)

3. The current king of the mountain—the Baby Boomers (born between 1945 and 1964)

In his book, *The Age Curve: How to Profit from the Coming Demographic Storm,*[1] Gronbach describes it as the "generational parade."

Every twenty years or so, the United States creates a new generation. Each generation is bound together by similar wants, needs, motives, and events. As they pass through time, all generations age and consume as they go.

In other words, there's a parade moving through our marketplace. But instead of marching, the parade is aging. Those at the front—the oldest—are already disbanding, while the youngest in the back of that parade are just now forming at the fairgrounds. The parade has a pace of its own and we can't slow it down, speed it up, or change the order of each section...

...for the most part the personality of the generation is determined by something very obvious: its size relative to the generation it follows.

So what are the personalities in the workplace?

Well, on a high level, the Boomers' mantra has always been a desire to change the world, and now that they are at the helm of the majority of today's American businesses, government, and education and religious institutions, that is exactly what they are endeavoring to do. They are willing to work hard because they like their fancy toys and big houses, but they are encumbered by situational ethics, and their time at the helm is limited with the progression of the parade—a sticky point for those who do not intend to grow old with grace.

The Gen Xers, on the other hand, have been labeled as entitled, lazy, and lacking in political participation, including voting and contributing to their political parties. However, a closer look reveals that they are not lazy (for the most part), they do vote, and they do participate politically; there are just fewer of them—11 percent fewer to be exact. There were 78.2 million Boomers and only 69.5 million Gen Xers, so they are entitled because of their size. They can insist on bringing their dogs to work and can just leave a job that doesn't suit their work-life balance picture because they can go get another job tomorrow—probably a better job that pays more. At least that has been the case until now....

Enter Gen Y.

Gen Y is a whole new ball game. They are a massive group, even larger than the Boomers, with an estimated 79.5 million members. They are entering the workforce as an organized, multi-tasking, techno-savvy mass that has demands of its own. According to Bruce Tulgan,[2] a founder of New Haven, Connecticut–based RainmakerThinking, Gen Y, "unlike the generations that have gone before them, has been pampered, nurtured and programmed with a slew of activities since they were toddlers, meaning they are both high-performance and high-maintenance." They are massive consumers and are used to having what they need and want. They are used to having their parents involved in every aspect of their lives, especially when the bill comes. And they, too, are entering the workforce somewhat entitled, but don't worry leaders. It won't last long. More on all this later.

So back to the employee/manager conference.... This is really just one small example of how the workplace is shifting at a sometimes mind-bending pace, and we have to learn how to lead and manage both the changes and the change makers. With the diverse generations, changes in technology, globalization, and competing agendas, the leaders of today and the future must be razor sharp and extremely adaptable.

To break down the issues effectively, we have divided this book into two sections. In the first section, we describe the diverse generations and shifting demographics, allowing you to gain an in-depth understanding of who they are and what they think about each other. In the second section, we will focus on how the demographic shift is impacting leadership and the overall workplace and provide some practical applications on how to deal with it.

Let's start with a look at our current business leaders.

Notes

1. Gronbach, Kenneth W. *The Age Curve: How to Profit from the Coming Demographic Storm.* New York: American Management Association, 2008. Print.

2. Armour, Stephanie. "Generation Y: They've Arrived at Work with a New Attitude." *USATODAY.com.* 08 Nov. 2005. Web. 24 July 2010. http://www.usatoday.com/money/workplace/2005-11-06-gen-y_x.htm.

Section I

Who are they and what do they think about each other?

Chapter 1 ——————————
Current Leaders in Charge

The research, while not exact, is very clear about the fact that the Boomers are currently at the helm. Statistics vary, but it doesn't take a research scientist to see which generation is overwhelmingly in charge of today's business world. If you look around, you'll see Boomers include most senior executives; the upper-level management tier in most organizations; the leadership of educational and religious institutions as well as the arts, sports, and entertainment; and, of course, governmental leaders.

It takes a lot of work to take the lead of so much of the world as we know it, and the Boomers certainly did—and are still doing—the work. In fact, they have embodied the term *workaholic*. Perhaps this is a trait picked up in the 60s when "other" addictions prevailed. Now they are addicted to work, power, fun, expensive toys, and probably a few things from back in the day as well.

The Boomers have had a profound impact on today's workplace and society in general, and they are still making their voice heard. In fact, they have finally made it to the platforms where they are both respected enough and powerful enough to make their mark on the world. They have for the most part been loyal to the organizations they've served, even when the organizations weren't loyal to them. They learned to compete fiercely with their peers in order to establish their place among their own extremely large generation; and, according to Tom Peters, they've single handedly made America (American women to be exact) the number one buying power in the world.

They like the power that work gives them, and while their generational parade may be coming to an end where work is concerned, don't expect them to quietly stop marching. As we speak, those who can are positioning themselves to go from the executive seat to the board seat. Some will need to keep working longer than expected. Others will transition to part-time and assume more of a mentorship role. Still others will move to community colleges to teach or local government, and of course, some will move to Florida and take up golf. But we can't forget that the Boomers have always had a voracious appetite for change and challenge, and they are not going to stop just because their parade scenery is changing. They want to feel needed and they want to continue to add value to the world, and we are going to need them to do just that. After all, the Boomers have some characteristics that we do not want to lose. Here are a few worth mentioning:

- They have a strong work ethic, while overdone, which has been one of their key contributions.

- They really understand doing what it takes when it's necessary, even if it is hard and takes a long time.

- They don't share everything all the time.

- They understand both the concept and the execution of strategy and are able to make difficult decisions when necessary.

- They do know how to share and are willing to share, but not if it means giving up their strategic position—that's just dumb.

- They typically prefer—and have often mastered the art of—face-to-face communication over e-mail and voice mail.

- They understand respect and protocol; after all, they learned from the best—the Silent Generation.

We would also like to hold on to their wisdom, and just as we never want John Travolta to stop dancing, we never want the Boomers to stop dreaming of making the world a better place, so we'd like to keep their idealism as well, please.

Of course, not all of their characteristics are exemplary. There are a few Boomer traits that we can stand to lose. For example, they took work ethic to an extreme. They made work their identity, often giving up their family and their health and sometimes their values for the work. As a group, they have big egos. Just like a big kid on the playground can be "king of the mountain," the Boomers have become "king of the mountain," and they aren't afraid to let the other kids know it.

While they do a good job with face-to-face communication, they also took the whole concept of meetings in the workplace to a new level, and now it's hard to get any production done at all in between all of the meetings.

We can also let go of the Boomers' situational "I meant it at the time" ethics. We've seen plenty of destruction from that phenomenon—think Bernie Madoff, Bernie Ebbers, Ken Lay... shall we go on?

They see the world as full of options, and therefore, they introduced constant change.

> It is a fact that the life of baby boomers was accompanied by postwar transformations changing the American society. The ideas about sexuality, gender, and family were altered profoundly. Likewise, parenthood changed, old age and retirement was redefined, and labor forces were transformed. Even in their old age, they seize opportunity to stay involved and active like staying in their work force to meet the responsibilities of supporting their children.[1]

So perhaps we could simplify and have a little less change. By the time organizations get their multimillion dollar technology platforms in place, they are already out of date. It seems like with all of the "options" and all of the "change" the Boomers brought to the world, they could get us some options for less toil and more time.

And while we're at it, Boomers can be a little difficult to relate to for the younger generations because they are so focused on their work. Don't interrupt them unless you can add value to the work. Even though they love change, they have only scratched the surface of implementing new technologies as if to say, "we didn't mean that much change." From all appearances, the Boomers are going to make just enough technological upgrades to get what they need to get the job done. Then when their workplace portion of the parade ends, they'll be all too happy to let Gen Xers bring in the new technology platforms with their massive price tags and outrageous interruptions to standard processes.

While it's no surprise that our current leaders add both positive and negative contributions to the workplace, what is a surprise is how unprepared we are for the next generation of leaders. In a survey of more than 400 HR executives from 40 countries by IBM in 2007, it was determined that more than three-quarters were concerned about their organization's ability to develop future leaders. This is an increasingly serious failure, given the backdrop of explosive growth in emerging markets and the retirement of experienced personnel, IBM warned.

Of course it isn't that these organizations *can't* develop future leaders. It is that they *haven't*; and with the Boomers retiring at a rate of one every 8 seconds, this is a problem.

You may be wondering how we got into this predicament? Well, we have to remember that Boomers consider themselves "...the timeless generation, often unwilling to let go of their youth," says Dr. Daniela Schreier, assistant professor of clinical counseling at The Chicago School. "It's a lingering characterization of their idealism and may account for trends like Botox and plastic surgery." Remember, when they hit 40, 40 became the new 30, and now that they are hitting 60, 60 is becoming the new 40. So if they see themselves as timeless, there's really no need to focus on the next generation of leaders. But as Gronbach says, the generational parade is moving forward whether the Boomers like it or not, and many organizations will have to play catch-up in developing the right level of next generation leaders to take the helm. "...Boomers are a big, complicated generation, but one thing can be said about them without fear of contradiction: They are no longer young."[2]

Notes

1.   Mitchell, Roger. "Impact of Baby Boomers on American Society." *EzineArticles*. EzineArticles.com, 2010. Web. 24 July 2010. http://ezinearticles.com/?Impact-of-Baby-Boomers-on-American-Society&id=932508.

2.   Brandon, Emily. "Generation Glum—Planning to Retire." *U.S. News & World Report LP*. 21 July 2008. Web. 24 July 2010. http://money.usnews.com/money/blogs/planning-to-retire/2008/07/21/generation-glum.

Chapter 2 —————————————

Being Led and Managed
by a Boomer Boss

While you're letting the concept of the changing of the guard soak in from the previous chapter, we'll share some very important tips on being led and managed by Boomers in this chapter. After all, the Boomers have been leaders in business, education, and government for many years now and they, along with Gen Xers, should have some wisdom to share with the younger Gen Y on the matter. So we will start with some Boomer boss basics.

The first time you will typically encounter your Boomer boss will be in the interview process. This could also be the last time if you don't interview well, so there are a few important things to remember, and these will also serve you well once you have landed the job:

1. First Impression
2. Effective Communication
3. Relentless Preparation
4. Sound Presentation
5. Speedy Execution
6. Follow-Through, Follow-Through, Follow-Through

1. **First impression.** Making a great first impression on a Boomer is not impossible, but as with anyone, you'll only have about 30 seconds to make your first impression. So you'll want that to go well. Here's the hot list of things to remember:

   a. **Be early.** Not on time—*early!* About 10 to 15 minutes early is perfect.

   b. Wait patiently. Don't fidget or sigh. Make your body language say you are calm and open. Mentally envision the interview going the way you want it to.

c. Turn off all electronic devices and act like they don't exist.

d. Be nice and informative to each person you encounter, especially administrative assistants. They are a part of the test at every level in the organization.

e. Dress one level above the dress attire for the position. If it is a professional environment, wear a suit. If it is business casual, dress at the high end of business casual. If it is casual, dress business casual. The Boomers have gone from bell-bottoms and long flowing dresses to all-out suits and then to business casual. When they came into the workforce, they learned in companies like IBM to dress professional with a dark suit, a white shirt, and a tie with a little red in it (for power). So it will serve you best to dress on the high end of what is required. Even if your Boomer boss is a casual person, he or she will appreciate the effort.

Now remember, all of these tips are excellent for your work with your Boomer boss, not just for the interview.

2. **Effective communication.** Communicating with your Boomer boss should start out formal. If he or she chooses to be more casual with you or ask you to be more casual, then you can adjust, but in the beginning, stay formal.

a. When you meet, stand to shake hands. Introduce yourself. Address him or her formally until given permission to do otherwise (Mr. Smith, Ms. Smith, Dr. Smith). While we're on that subject, do *not* make the mistake of not knowing whether or not your Boomer boss has a doctorate. He or she has worked hard for an advanced degree and the title that goes with it, so don't forget to use it.

b. Wait to sit until asked or gestured to do so.

c. Do not be afraid to make a little small talk while transitioning into a meeting, but remember, even the small talk will be subtly evaluated, so be careful what you choose as a topic. For instance, "What do you think about our president?" is not a good question to start with. On the other hand, "I see you received your doctorate from _____. What made you choose that school?" is a good question; it's relevant (to work) and shows interest in him or her (you can never go wrong with that!).

d. Do not, we repeat, *do not,* look at your phone during a meeting. In fact, turn it off or silence it. Your full attention is expected.

e. Allow your Boomer boss to lead the conversation, but answer thoroughly and ask relevant questions as the opportunity allows. Don't interrupt. It's rude and shows a lack of discipline.

f. Listen carefully. If you give your full attention to the conversation, listening should come easily. Try to listen for understanding without weighing whether or not you agree with what is being said.

g. Follow up on statements you make and be aware of your body language. If you say you are going to send your Boomer boss something during a meeting, be sure to write it down and send it immediately after the interview. At the same time, your body language must communicate your openness and self-assuredness. No one wants to have an employee who seems insecure and all locked up.

h. Don't waste time. Your Boomer boss has work to do, and if your meeting isn't contributing to what he or she has to get done, your Boomer boss will want to wrap up quickly.

i. Give answers in sequence, even using numbers if applicable. For example, if he or she asks you about your contributions to date, you might say, "I believe I've had four major contributions in my work so far: (1) I've mastered the Spanish language, which positively impacted my work here by...; (2) I've located two additional revenue streams from an existing product; (3) I've lowered expenses in my area by…; and (4) I've united my work team through…."

j. Before you leave, make sure that both you and your Boomer boss know exactly who is responsible for action items and when action items are due. In addition, make and confirm the assignments of any other follow-ups. Don't leave things hanging that will require another meeting or e-mail later. You both have enough to do already.

k. At the end of a meeting, stand, shake hands again, and get back to work.

3. **Relentless preparation.** Remember, for your Boomer boss, life is work, so arriving unprepared because of having to take your child to school or other such matters will not be appreciated. Your Boomer boss will think you should have prepared before last-minute changes would interrupt your plans. Preparing is one thing; preparing with excellence is a better thing. Don't just prepare, over-prepare. Know more than you need to know and have back-up data as well. Be well researched and thorough. Besides, for your own sake, great preparation will give you a lot of self-confidence when you get ready to present your case or project.

4. **Sound presentation.** Speaking of presentation, this is a lot like making a strong first impression. The presentation of your case or project is a part of the equation in order to be successful with your Boomer boss. If you have made a good initial impression, communicated well, and over-prepared, but you make your case on sloppy materials, PowerPoint slides, or spreadsheets, you will lose credibility. In addition, your verbal presentation will play an important part. When presenting to your Boomer boss, speak clearly and with openness. Be forthright but don't give more details than necessary to make your point; however, have the details for the drill of questioning that is bound to follow. It's a good idea to practice. While you're driving in to work the morning of the

presentation, go over some of the important points to make sure you have your thoughts in order before you ever open your mouth at the meeting.

5. **Speedy execution.** While the Boomers lived through the 70s, not many of them still live the 70s lifestyle, so don't expect them to be slow and laid back. You can do everything else right, but if you fail to execute the plan in a timely manner, your Boomer boss will lose confidence quickly. If you say you can get something done, get it done and have it done by the deadline. Excuses may be listened to by your Boomer boss, but each excuse weakens your credibility. It is a good idea to give your Boomer boss as much feedback as possible throughout the process so that he or she knows if it is going in the right direction or the wrong direction. Of course there will be times when your project or assignment fails—that is just part of business. The best way to keep the faith is to look your Boomer boss in the eye and say "Here's what happened. Here's where I personally failed. Here's where the team failed. Here's what we are going to do about it." More than likely, your Boomer boss will roll up his or her sleeves and help you start over or move to the next step. The Boomer boss understands the concept of going to battle when necessary and is not afraid to get his or her hands dirty when the work is difficult.

6. **Follow-through, follow-through, follow-through.** In every area of work, follow-through separates the good from the excellent. You can have the talent of a B-player, but if you establish great follow-through skills and add a lot of heart to your work, you can improve your grade with your Boomer boss. Great follow-through is more than just following up on a task; it's following up on the follow-up. Just take it one more step: it will set you far apart from your peers, and you'll make life better for you and for your Boomer boss.

Of course every Boomer boss is different, so please realize we are sharing generalizations here. It will be critical that you read the situation and learn the personal preferences of your Boomer boss in order to be successful.

One last tip: Whatever you do, don't make the mistake of trying to get around your Boomer boss in your career path. Remember, life is work for them, and they are more than willing to go to battle to hold their strategic position, and if that means a few casualties in the process, well... so be it.

Chapter 3 ——————————
Leading and Managing Boomers

Now working for a Boomer boss is one thing, but having a Boomer work for you is another. With the generational parade progressing steadily along, the shift in leadership is inevitable. The Boomers have led the charge for a long time, and many are continuing to lead, but those who have not continued to learn and grow are finding that the workplace and all of its technological innovations are passing the skills of yesteryear with breakneck speed. Many will soon find that they no longer have the skills or capabilities to lead today's departments, business units, or organizations, but don't expect them to admit it.

Some of this will take care of itself with the Boomers retiring at a rate of one every 8 seconds, but the economic turmoil combined with their never-grow-old attitude may have many Boomers delaying retirement plans until they are literally forced off the workplace playground by younger generations. One writer put it like this:

> Welcome, Baby Boomers. In another year or two you're going to start retiring and joining us old folks. You better get ready. After all these decades of being the toast of the town, the biggest-ever generation to whom attention must be paid, you're about to become passé. *Or not.*[1]

We think, not.... It doesn't have to be an ugly scene. There is a win/win/win scenario, and we just have to find it. Remember, Boomers have a lot of characteristics we like, and even more importantly, they have learned wisdom from the years in the trenches *and* they have the workplace knowledge and product intelligence that are needed to minimize strategic mistakes as innovation and technology take their place. Just as Minnesota employers are mapping ways to tap their experience—and to accommodate those who want to stay on the job[2]—we can do this inside our organizations. For example, we can try the following:

- Create transitional retirement plans, allowing Boomers to have more time off or shorter work weeks while remaining an important part of the team. They'll have more time to play with the grandkids, travel, play golf, work on their hobbies or start another small business.

- Provide Boomers with a career coach who can help them reinvent themselves within the organization to continue to add value, which is very important to the Boomers, and also to continue to earn a paycheck to keep up their big houses and expensive toys (and now the expensive toys for their grandkids).

- Create consultant contracts for retiring Boomers to consult back to the organization on an as-needed basis, bringing in their long-term expertise when needed, yet moving their big salaries off of payroll.

We're sure there are many more options, and every employer and Boomer can begin to come up with scenarios that fit his/her environment. Just remember, "Boomers are pro-environmental, anti-war, root for the under dog, change the worlders."[3] Surely there's something in your company that can benefit from these characteristics.

All this is sort of logistics, and it's fun to think about the new options the world is creating that Boomers will love, because they love options and they love change. However, there is a less fun side to the leadership transition, and that is the common scenario taking place every day in the workplace: a Boomer, for one reason or another, is moved under an Xer boss or, God forbid, a Y boss.

Yes, we know: the more sophisticated workplaces have this all figured out and are moving to more of a team-based model—it's like one big happy family. It's just that our experience paints another scenario, so let's spend some time getting the issues out on the table:

- For Boomers, their life is or has been their work for a long time.

- Boomers have fought long and worked hard to get to the "king of the mountain" position.

- Author Howard Smead says that Boomers are "the most egocentric generation in the history of mankind."

- Boomers can be very competitive and sometimes hard to please.[4]

Now, take these characteristics in an employee and move that employee to where he or she is working for someone younger, possibly half his or her age. Sometimes this happens in a company where the Boomer has worked the majority of his or her career and feels that he or she has a lot more value to add than the new, younger boss. Don't expect Boomers to take it lying down. You are going to encounter one of two types of Boomer employees: pessimistic or optimistic. Here's how one person described these two types:

> I've been talking to a lot of my boomer friends lately to wish them well over the holidays. Some are morbid and pessimistic and keep complaining about the inability to retire. Others are youthful and optimistic, constantly seeking BOTOX® as their spa-replacement solution.[5]

Either way, it's happening, so the younger generations are going to have to learn how to deal with it. This is a good place to apply some of the lessons we've learned from Boomers.

While it may not be an easy situation, it is not an impossible one either. Boomers may be tough competitors with big egos, but they are able to wrap their arms around new challenges, so engage them in the process of figuring out how best to work together. Don't be offended if the first stab at this is more like "just let me do my work and we'll get along fine." You may also sense some unspoken tension as everyone learns to deal with the new situation. It's going to take a little effort on everyone's parts to get this ball rolling in the right direction. Here are a few ways to move through the tough spots with your Boomer employees:

1. Don't come in waving your title around and saying effectively, "I'm the boss now, so we're going to do it my way." Come in softly, but not timidly. You'll need strength, courage, and confidence to lead well in today's workplace.

2. While you don't want to "pull rank," you also don't want to drag out the transition. Dragging out this process doesn't help anyone and creates ambiguity. Move swiftly into the leadership position, but be an open-minded leader who is able to learn from employees. Ask questions: gain an understanding of the people and their communication preferences, work styles, skills, etc.

3. Be clear about what is expected of you and what you expect from them, and whenever possible, give them options.

4. Answer the Boomers' questions thoroughly and don't be surprised if you get grilled for details. It's not personal; it's just their way.

5. Put the right people in the right places regardless of age. Whether they are a Boomer, an X, or a Y, they still have to show themselves worthy of the position. When a person is underperforming, even if that person is twice your age, you still have to manage his or her performance and help him or her get on the right track or move that person to another track/position inside or outside of the company. The rules don't change just because the person you're managing may be old enough to be your parent.

6. Respect the Boomers' work ethic. It isn't likely that you'll have to ask them to work harder. The Boomers understand hard work, and whatever time they have on the job, they will be glad to spend it doing meaningful work. On the other hand, if they are not valued, it's going to be an

ugly scene for everyone: you'll lose their idealism and see their cynical side, which isn't pretty from any generation.

7. Prove yourself to your Boomer employee with results. Do what you say you are going to do, when you say you are going to do it, and do it consistently. Don't spend too much time talking about the work. Show them your ability, and you'll gain credibility and their trust over time.

> *Effective leadership is not about making speeches or being liked; leadership is defined by results not attributes.*
>
> — **Peter Drucker**

By focusing on getting results in a collaborative way with a positive attitude you are very likely to win over your Boomer employee. It's an ego tester all the way around, but if you create an environment where each person is appreciated for the role that he or she plays, it can be both fun and exciting.

> *Your character is more important than your position.*
>
> *Respect is earned, not demanded.*

Stay focused on the kind of person you want to be, not the title or position. You'll know you've done a good job when age is mentioned and you and your Boomer employee can both honestly say, "It's never a factor."

Notes

1. Stock, Robert W. "Baby Boomers, Here's What's Coming Next." *AOL News.* AOL Inc. Web. 24 July 2010.

2. Totten, Sanden. "Age and Experience Count against Older Workers | Minnesota Public Radio NewsQ." *Minnesota Public Radio.* MPR News, 19 June 2008. Web. 24 July 2010. http://minnesota.publicradio.org/display/web/2008/06/16/older wkrsunemployment/.

3. Viscusi, Stephen. "Interview Tips on How to Be 'Perceived' as 10 Years Younger than You Really Are on an Interview." *Generation Integration: Roberta Matuson Unites Boomers, X-ers and Millennials in the Workplace.* 20 Dec. 2009. Web. 24 July 2010. http://generationintegration.typepad.com/ matuson/2009/12/interview-tips-on-how-to-be-perceived-as-10- years-younger-than-you-really-are-on-an-interview.html.

4. Zust, Christine W. "Baby Boomer Leaders Face Challenges by Christine W. Zust—EmergingLeader.com." *EmergingLeader. com | Exploring Strategies and Concepts of Leadership through User Participation, Articles, Links, Profiles, Discussions and More.* Web. 24 July 2010. http://www.emergingleader.com/ article16.shtml.

5. Ko, Lina. "Get Brain-Fit In the New Year." *Boomerwatch.ca.* 18 Dec. 2009. Web. 24 July 2010. http://www.boomerwatch.ca/ ?p=382.

Chapter 4 ————————————

Changing of the Guard—
Boomers to Gen Xers

Let's turn our attention to the next generation of leaders who will run our corporations, educational and religious institutions, the arts, sports and entertainment industries, and the government in the coming decades. The parade scene is definitely changing with the Boomers retiring at the rate of one every 8 seconds. The last of the Boomers will turn 65 by the year 2029. In addition, there are 11 percent fewer Gen Xers than Boomers, and Gen Xers are the next group in line to take the leadership helm. However, the Boomers have been slow and sometimes negligent in the development of this up-and-coming generation. There are definitely some organizations that are doing an excellent job of developing next-generation leaders with both formal and informal high-potential programs, so we are not making a blanket failure statement here, just pointing out a clear gap in our upcoming leadership capabilities.

There is some good news in all of this: there is still time in most organizations. With the Boomers drawing out the retirement process with plans that include phased retirement and contracting back to the company, we can start where we are and develop strong leaders for the inevitable changing of the guard in the generational parade.

More good news: as Gronbach points out in *The Age Curve*,[1] the shortage of midlevel managers will avail unprecedented opportunity to minorities and immigrants to advance their careers. Latinos and African Americans will find that common-place racial barriers to corporate advancement will no longer exist as they become a hot commodity for leadership advancement both due to the gap in available leaders and also due to our need and desire to create more diverse leadership teams across the nation. We can measure our success when every research report on leaders in America is no longer 70 percent white middle-aged male. We've had that for the past 200 years. It's time to move on, America.

Who They Are

Gen X has had an interesting path that has shaped this generation into "...a generation of nomads," as Dr. Schreier says. "Many never settle down into a job or a relationship. They adapt easily to new situations, but they also feel torn, like they are always floating and wondering 'where do I belong?'"[2] This group is marked by independence. They want it their way (think Burger King). They are somewhat irreverent, cynical, and indifferent—often refusing to live by corporate or societal rules. They question everything, including what is ethical and who made it that way. They want choices and that includes career choices. They typically have very little loyalty to the organizations they work for. They move from place to place, looking for a settlement that fits their desired lifestyle, but they never really settle.

Gen Xers like jobs with flexible hours and insist on work-life balance. They're the ones who want to bring their dogs to work and take off for every child or family event. They are the first generation to fully embrace the Internet, and they are eager to use it in ways that fit their idea of work, such as easier telecommuting, video conferencing, and anything else that gives them increased independence.

> Gen Xers tend to be impatient, to put a high value on their time, and to show little tolerance for having it wasted. They show little respect for authority. Doubting tradition is a virtue, a way of engaging for them. They were certainly not taught using "rote" memorization. They do not focus well on "logical steps" leading to a conclusion. The print medium that encouraged linear thinking is not their medium. They are more comfortable with one-on-one training, coaching and mentoring.[3]

Gen Xers want to have it all. They came into their own professionally where "in the Roaring 90s, people seemed proud of their idiocy. Consumption turned into a religion, growth seemed endless, new industries were popping up everywhere, and armchair philosophers were given a global voice in the form of America Online and other similar services."[4]

It was quite a ride. Money for nice cars and big mortgages and any halfway viable .net idea came easy. This generation ran up huge debts with little or no thought about paying them back. "I'll just get another loan or shift money from one low-interest credit card to the other." Imagine their shock when it all came crashing down in 2008 and 2009. Of course they weren't alone; the Boomers participated in this money bubble as well. Regardless, it seems the age of arrogance is over, and the Gen Xers can no longer over-ego-ly maneuver from one high-paying job to another. For the first time, Gen Xers are celebrating when their peers get a job—any job. Welcome to the real world, Gen X.

And it doesn't stop there. Gen Y is coming in one big massive force, and if they've seen their ride to the top as fairly straight forward, apparently they haven't looked in the rearview mirror. There is an enormous, focused, goal-oriented throng of achievers coming around their back left fender, and if they don't want to get passed, they better be sure that they are *very* engaged in the race.

On top of all that, the "timeless" Boomers won't leave fast enough for some ambitious Gen Xers. So now they are facing new competition for the top seats, the seemingly inevitable bankruptcy of Social Security, disappearance of Medicare, shifting healthcare, and waning retirement plans in the face of their massive debt load that they have acquired during the Roaring 90s. So to use a Haitian phrase, they have "mountains beyond mountains" or problems beyond problems. But all is not lost.

Redeeming Qualities

Gen X has many redeeming qualities. In spite of their carelessness with their finances when it came to acquiring debt, "...it turns out that they're more philanthropic than older generations. A new survey from Northern Trust found that Gen X millionaires give nearly twice as much, on average, to charitable causes as their elders. Gen X households are also more generous in their intended charitable bequests, planning to give 22 percent of their estate to charity, compared with 16 percent for Boomers and 14 percent for silent generation millionaires." [5]

This generation is also quickly dispensing with common stereotypes around gender and race. You'll find Gen Xers shaking their heads or simply being aghast at prejudice and archaic mind-sets. Of course, they are not without their own prejudices: the new elite are those who embrace globalization, multiculturalism, and liberalism. It doesn't make their prejudices any better, just different. Perhaps not having any prejudices would be against human nature and just asking too much.

Gen Xers also love to learn, and they like work to be interesting. They are good at working independently and actually thrive when allowed to do so. They rarely settle for the status quo. They are typically competent and techno savvy. They are quite entrepreneurial. Their independence and irreverence for the old way of doing things have brought us the dot.com boom and the dot.com bust as well as the mortgage boom and the mortgage bust. They aren't afraid to step out and try new things, even radical things such as new business models that do not require a profit. OK, so that wasn't so smart, but hey, at least they are trying some new things. Out of these failures, there are many successes such as... and..., okay, give us a minute. Something will come to us.

Just a little joke, don't write us letters. Seriously, Gen X has created some great new brands like Google, Amazon, Yahoo, and eBay. They have also proven to be a lot less lazy than originally thought. "The United States has more billionaires under 40 than at any other time in history, and author Bruce Tulgan estimates that Gen Xers create four out of every five new enterprises.

> Unexpectedly, generation X is bringing that same entre- preneurial, pragmatic spirit to social ills, creating an array of nonprofit and for-profit organizations to tackle problems. So these past years have brought forth a cadre of new, gen X leaders who have founded promis- ing new ventures.[6]

On the home front, they have definitely had a positive impact. They've reinvented parent involvement and taken it to a whole new level. If there is one thing the children of Gen Xers are not it is abandoned. Gen Xers are determined to make up for the lack of work-life balance their parents had and, in doing so, have become the most involved parents on record. They may be indif- ferent about work at times, but they are never indifferent about their children, and we'll see this play out further when we dive into Gen Y.

How Did They Become Who They Are?

With such an interesting mix of characteristics, you may wonder why Gen X is so different than Boomers. Well, for one thing, they were one of the "least parented" generations ever: 40 percent were latchkey kids, and half of their parents divorced. This factor has lead some to an extreme of advocating for their children even to the detriment of the group.[7]

Gen Xers grew up in a society that was largely influenced and run by Boomers whose intense lives they often reacted against. Many found their "liberated" parents focused on careers and causes at the expense of families. Their parents had the highest divorce rates in history. Most Gen X kids grew up in single-parent or double-income homes. The child-rearing theory of the day stressed giving kids decision-making power and "not stifling them with rules." Without a high level of nurturing and emotional bonding, they became skeptical, with an inclination to be inde- pendent. Some were forced into adult roles in dysfunctional families. Gen Xers were growing up during the deterioration of social, religious, political, and business institutions, which contributed to their disillusionment and distrust of authority.[8]

This lack of parenting led to a sort of generational "street smarts" where Gen Xers learned to do things on their own and made up their own independent rules as they went. Looking back over the Gen X foundation, it's really no surprise that they learned to depend on themselves, decided work wasn't everything, delayed getting married, bought their own homes, and looked for ways to remain primarily untethered except for child rearing where, determined to be different, they created a whole new category: over parenting.

Gen X's "tough" street-savvy independence has kept them alive in the shadow of the older Boomers, but it hasn't always created a beautiful working relationship. In fact, being managed by and being the manager of Gen X is no small endeavor for even the most seasoned Boomer leaders not to mention their fellow Gen Xers or the younger Gen Y. Let's take a look....

Notes

1.   Gronbach, Kenneth W. *The Age Curve: How to Profit from the Coming Demographic Storm.* New York: American Management Association, 2008. Print.

2.   "Psychology Across the Generations." *INSIGHT Magazine.* Dec. 2009. Web. 24 July 2010. http://insight-magazine.org/2009/headline/psychology-across-the-generations/.

3.   Multhauf, Carmen and Lloyd. "Gen X IS the Market." *RISMedia Real Estate News | Industry Trends | Marketing— Residential & Commercial.* 28 Oct. 2008. Web. 23 July 2010. http://rismedia.com/2008-10-27/gen-x-is-the-market/.

4.   Azzurro, Frank. "Why the Bad Economy Is Good for Productive People." *Amerika.* 19 Dec. 2009. Web. 23 July 2010. http://www.amerika.org/2009/globalism/why-the-bad-economy-is-good-for-productive-people.

5.   Marquardt, Katy. "When It Comes to Giving, Gen X Trumps Boomers." *U.S. News & World Report.* 8 Sept. 2008. Web. 23 July 2010. http://www.usnews.com/money/blogs/new-money/2008/09/08/when-it-comes-to-giving-gen-x-trumps-boomers.

6.   Gergen, David. "Shattering Expectations." *U.S. News & World Report.* Money & Business, 11 Dec. 2005. Web. 24 July 2010. http://www.usnews.com/usnews/biztech/ articles/051219/19gergen.htm.

7.   Ring, Sara. "Are Gen X Parents a Pain, or a Plus?" *K–12 Education & Learning Innovations with Proven Strategies That Work.* The Edutopia Poll. Web. 24 July 2010. http://www.edutopia.org/poll-generation-x-parents.

8.   Multhauf, Carmen and Lloyd. "Gen X IS the Market." *RISMedia Real Estate News | Industry Trends | Marketing— Residential & Commercial*. 28 Oct. 2008. Web. 23 July 2010. http://rismedia.com/2008-10-27/gen-x-is-the-market/.

Chapter 5

Being Led and Managed by a Gen Xer

Gen Xers will definitely have a chance to prove that they can be effective leaders, but only time will tell for sure. One problem that Gen Xers will face as leaders is that they are not like either the Boomers or Gen Y. They are sandwiched between these two massive generations, and they are fundamentally out of tune with both. They want to be and were somewhat forced to be independent from the older Boomers, and that very independence makes them out of step with the very team-based Gen Y. However, Gen Xers have some qualities that may make them truly able to step up to the challenge of leadership roles that will eventually be placed on their independent shoulders.

So what do those being managed by Gen X need to know? Well, just as with any boss, there will be good and bad, and which way it is weighted depends on the individual leader. However, on a macro level, you can count on your Gen X boss to be very clear about desired results, expectations, and how results will be measured. He or she will care a great deal about doing a good job, because doing a good job makes a person employable. Gen Xers are very focused on being employable. They will care about their own title and yours, but not because they want the title. They are only interested in a title that makes sense on their career path and that gives them a logical upward progression. After all, they do need to make as much money as possible, because many Gen Xers got themselves in trouble with subprime mortgages and other easy money that they consumed with gusto and now have to figure out how to repay.

Your Gen X boss will look for creative and even entrepreneurial solutions, regardless of the size of the organization you are working in, and will be delighted when you do the same. Because of their fierce independence, Gen Xers will lead the way, but may at times forget that anyone is following. Independence is a characteristic that doesn't just go away because they become leaders. They will work hard with complete commitment to getting results, but they may also take the whole team to a baseball game on Thursday afternoon to give everyone's mind a break and rejuvenate creativity. They are not stuck in the conventional, and for them, this type of outing is just as much a part of work as sitting in front of the computer. Creativity comes out of play more than it does out of work.

You might think that your Gen X boss doesn't need much appreciation due to his/her independent nature, but you would be making a big mistake. Gen Xers will be as generous as possible with their employees when it comes to financial reward, work location, flex schedules, etc., as they learn how to lead, but if their generosity isn't appreciated, they will be hurt and will pull back to lick their wounds and watch their backs like they always have.

Of course that doesn't mean that you'll always hear a lot of appreciation from your Gen X boss. It isn't that they don't appreciate their employees; they are just so busy trying to work and focus on family at the same time that they sometimes forget to give positive feedback to their employees. A little reminder now and then is good for Gen Xers, and they are likely to respond with genuine appreciation both for the feedback and for the good work you have provided.

If you are a high producer, you may hear little from your Gen X boss. Gen Xers love low-maintenance, high-producing employees and may think that the way to reward them is to let them do their work their own way. This management style is great for some and a real problem for others who desire more structure and a steady stream of feedback. Gen Y's need for constant feedback will most likely exhaust Gen X bosses.

Gen X also has strong survival skills, so if a project or company is in trouble, your Gen X boss will most likely jump in and try to help. Gen Xers may be skeptical, but they are also creative and entrepreneurial, so don't expect them to throw in the towel when the going gets tough. Put on the coffee and prepare for some late-night, sleeves-rolled-up problem solving.

If a company or project fails, your Gen X boss will most likely keep everything in perspective. Hopefully no one died, and everything else is secondary to that. It is OK to admit failure to your Gen X boss, but it isn't OK to spend too much time crying about it and it isn't OK to point the finger at someone else—ever. The best thing to do if you make a mistake is to own it, accept all or partial responsibility, try to make right what you can, and wait for the response. Just tell it like it is: Gen X can take it. On the other hand, if the failure is due to organizational policies and politics beyond the control of Gen Xers, they will barely be able to cover their disgust and may be seen swearing under their breath when they run up against institutional bureaucracy, a lack of technology, and other such obstacles.

As a group, Gen Xers will have little tolerance for race or gender discrimination since they have grown up in a mixed-race America and the global economy has taken shape during their entrance into the workforce. They look at today's organizations with surprise and some disgust that there are not more people of color or women at the top. They'll go about changing this scene with vigor, and by the time Gen Y takes the "king of the mountain" position, we should see the national melting pot displayed at the top of our organizations—if we even have a traditional top of the organization then. So if you are a minority or a woman, you should not find these characteristics to be a barrier in your career under your Gen X boss. Let's hope Gen X remembers tolerance when it comes to age....

Now Gen Xers love technology, even if they don't always understand it, so technological advances will flourish under their reign. If you have technology ideas that fit within the budget or you can prove a positive return-on-investment, your Gen X boss will take you seriously. This generation will be willing to try new things with technology and see how it goes. Gen Xers are used to technology causing as many problems as it fixes and, at times, bringing about delays in work. They know that this is part of the price for change and are tolerant, though impatient, with technologically progressive thinking.

Your Gen X boss will also be very open to your using social networking sites as well as in-person networking to move your work forward. They are very adept at this themselves and can be tapped for connections when needed. Gen X bosses will pride themselves on connections. They'll love it when you ask them for a connection and they are able to provide it. They learned not to burn bridges and they know how to reach across, backwards, and forwards in their network. Top Gen X networkers know how to create an opening into a contact or organization in seconds. This is one place their resourcefulness will help you as their employee and the organization that you work for.

Your Gen X boss will also be very open with you about your career. You will be allowed and often encouraged to voice aspirations to leave your current position or even organization. Your Gen X boss will even help you achieve your career goals, but only if you are worth the investment (read "if you are a low-maintenance high producer"). Of course helping you with your career could someday come back around to help your Gen X boss with his or her own career, so he or she is not likely to burn any bridges, even if you are not exactly a low-maintenance high producer.

Your Gen X boss will also completely understand if you prefer to leave your job to stay home to raise your children. This makes perfect sense to your Gen X boss, and he or she will not look down on parents who are returning to the workforce after a time at home with the kids. Remember, Gen Xers are the ones involved in every aspect of their children's lives, so they value this trait in others as well. However, this can get a little sketchy for Gen Xers when they are in a middle-management position in an organization that does not value such work-life balance. They'll do their best to help you with this, but realize their success may depend on "butts in seats," and if so, there is only so much they can do and remain highly valued and employable.

Another positive about working for Gen Xers is that they will be keenly aware of humanitarian and environment issues. They will reach across the world when possible to impact fellow human beings with difficult living environments, and they will love to participate in everything "green." The Boomers started the race in this phenomenon, and Gen X is proudly reaching for the baton, excited to make a difference in the world through everyday, realistic choices. Your Gen X boss will love it when you contribute to the effort with both actions and ideas.

Overall, Gen Xers have everything to gain and nothing to lose as they move into the "king of the mountain" position. As leaders, they will most likely struggle with conventional, workaholic Boomers as they question just about everything that is and ask "Why?" If it doesn't make sense to them, they'll set about trying to change it and hopefully will not crash too many things in the process (.com boom, .com bust; mortgage boom, mortgage bust). Gen X leaders will also face the mirror as they learn to lead other Gen Xers. Picture two dogs' teeth on a toy, looking eye to eye and pulling in opposite directions—not because they need to go in opposite directions but because it's just their nature to be stubborn and resistant.

This will be a learning experience in itself.

Gen Xers leading Gen Y will be interesting, exciting, difficult, awkward at times, and overall unconventional. Where Gen Xers thought they were bringing the world into the 21st century kicking and screaming, they'll find that they are the ones kicking and screaming when Gen Y kicks workplace change into supersonic.

Chapter 6 ——————————

Leading and Managing Gen X

While it's been going on for some time, leading and managing Gen X has seemingly just hit the radar and primarily only because of the impending leader gap. Sometimes, lost in the masses, Gen X is a sandwich generation—sandwiched between two enormous generations. Recruiters went from recruiting and retaining Boomers to recruiting and retaining Gen Y with barely a passing glance at Gen Xers. Are they being passed over? Well, no, not exactly, but like Dr. Suess's Whos in *Horton Hears a Who!*[1] they are going to have to work hard to make their voices heard.

The very idea of "management" of Gen X may be inappropriate as they will all too quickly let you know that the better term is "lead." And what does it take to be a leader of Gen X? The same thing it takes to be a leader of anyone—followers. But whom will independent Gen X follow?

The best place to start is probably with flexibility. Leading Gen X will require flexibility, so today's leaders can become more flexible voluntarily or by force, but either way, they will become more flexible. Gen Xers are not going to work well for those who micromanage, who are sticklers for the "clock," or who fear loss of productivity just because they are working virtually versus in their cubicle or their "officle" (a cubicle with a door—it offers all the downsides of a cube with none of the advantages of an office, except for the door).

While they are not very trusting, Gen Xers do really want to be trusted by their managers when it comes to whether or not they are doing their work. It could be a sticky situation, but it doesn't have to be. While they want to be trusted, they also don't mind being measured by results. Therefore the **Results-Only Workplace Environment (ROWE**[2]) is tailor-made for Gen X. In fact, it was probably Gen X that came up with it.

If you have not encountered ROWE yet, it basically means just what it says. There are no set hours; there is no sick leave or vacation leave. Employees work where they want and when they want. The only thing that gets measured is results: no results, no job.

Some of the foremost leaders in the ROWE movement, **CultureRX** says "cubicles, desktop computers, and phones with cords will soon be the workplace relics of our time—just like the mimeograph machine, While You Were Out pink slips, and typewriters are of the Industrial Age workplace….

Benefits include:

- **Productivity.** Get more work from existing workforce now

- **Retention.** Keep the talent you want; say goodbye to the talent that isn't producing results

- **Attraction.** Be a magnet for the best talent from all generations

- **Elimination of wasteful practices.** Elimination of unnecessary tasks and processes; communication becomes more efficient and effective

- **A workforce that's fluid, flexible, and accountable.** Ability to perform in a more agile, 24/7 manner with clear, measurable goals for every employee

- **Optimization of space.** No need for 1:1 workspace requirements or hoteling programs

- **Life balances for all.** Environment that is inclusive and fair without the headache of managing a flexible work program

- **Improved employee engagement/morale/loyalty.** Happy employees boost the bottom line, are more dedicated, and produce better results

- **Go green.** Reduce your impact on the environment by creating a culture where everyone uses common sense about where they get work done—whether from home, a coffee shop or library. Wherever. Whenever."

> *In my ten-plus years as a manager, I have never seen a tool that more effectively or completely unleashes the power of employees to focus on customers or that sets the stage for eliminating waste, motivating teams, or for attracting and retaining talent better than ROWE. It is the one tool that I believe is absolutely essential to be a good manager and that companies need to have in-house to be competitive.*
>
> **— Certified Black Belt, Lean Six Sigma**
> **www.culturerx.com**[3]

Work done when you want, where you want with built-in work-life balance and success based on results: now that's what Gen X was born for. However, most of the workplaces in America have not yet made this audacious jump, so we really must talk about managing and leading Gen X from a more (cough, cough) "traditional" standpoint.

During a leadership retreat for a large physician group, Hagemann encountered a jaw-dropping phenomenon among Gen X physicians. Now Hagemann is a seasoned leadership development professional who has worked with all levels of leaders for many years, so causing her jaw to drop is really not that easy to do, but none-the-less, here's what happened. The retreat, facilitated by Hagemann, was designed to get the right people in the right positions in the organization. The physician group had about 30 physicians and annual revenue of approximately $50 million as a part of a large healthcare network. The group had grown quickly and entrepreneurially and ultimately established itself as a high-priority department in the network. Because of the quick growth rate, more structure was becoming a necessity. Those who were in leadership were usually there because they were the best technicians, and the section chiefs were usually the best clinical physicians. The only problem is to be great technically or clinically does not necessarily make a person a good leader. In fact, several of these professionals had gone from being A-players as technicians or physicians to B- or C-players as leaders.

So Hagemann led the group through a series of steps that involved removing the names, determining appropriate positions for the current and future leadership needs, and then trying to figure out who the potential leaders were for the newly designed or aligned positions. The work was fairly swift when it came to the technicians (probably because they weren't at the meeting), but when it came to the physicians, the jaw-dropping began.

First, there was only one physician out of 30 who really wanted to be a leader. There was another who was willing to *be* a leader, but was not willing to *do* anything that leadership requires. None were willing to give up their eight weeks of vacation or to take on the potential evening work or even check e-mail after hours since they were typically off work by 4:00 p.m.

In addition, the Gen X physicians had a lot of complaints about the current leadership not communicating enough. They claimed there was a conspiracy to leave them out of decision making by not telling them when the meetings were or allowing them to have a voice. A little digging revealed that the current leaders were, in fact, informative. They sent notices about meetings via e-mail *and* posted notices in the offices. The problem was that the physicians didn't feel that checking e-mail was part of their job and didn't notice the posted notices. They definitely weren't going to check e-mail after work, because they had to walk their dogs (yes, they said that). And some of the male physicians wreaked havoc on the rotation schedule by scheduling time off from work in order to take their wives to gynecologist appointments.

Is your jaw dropping yet? Ultimately, this group ended up with the chief and the one physician who wanted to be a leader taking most of the leadership responsibility and arranging the rest of the organization to fit that model. It won't work long term, but it won't have to. This is nothing a little healthy competition won't fix. In the next few years, Gen Y should start getting out of med school, and even the high-paid physicians will have to grow up and do some things that they do not want to do like the rest of the Gen Xers—you know the ones celebrating when their friends get a job—any job.

This story confirms that managing and leading Gen X can seem like a daunting task in a traditional environment. Still, it can be done with some awareness and ability to flex your own style in order to meet theirs, at least for now.

Leaders will have to keep Gen Xers' independent nature in mind when managing this generation. While the Boomers banned together to change the world, Gen X is not exactly the most team-oriented group you will encounter. It is not that they are anti-team, it's just that "...the team effort most Boomers envision, Claire Raines says, is more like football, in which every member acts in concert. For Gen X, it's more like a relay race: 'I'll give it all I've got—when and where I'm supposed to.'"[4]

So leaders can start by honoring Gen Xers' sense of independence and being flexible about how and when they do the work. Leaders may not understand Gen Xers, but they can at least try to express support of Gen Xers' desire to have work-life balance. (Eye-rolling not allowed.) In addition to a flexible work environment, Gen X loves to learn. Leaders will be able to keep them pretty happy by providing them with ample opportunities to learn and develop. Leaders can use this to the company's advantage by giving them learning opportunities that in turn solve problems and create solutions for the organization. Gen Xers love to be a part of the solution, so the more they are involved in problem solving, the better their chances are of having a future with the company.

Boomer bosses may be surprised to find that Gen X is not as focused on climbing the ladder as Boomers are. We've even encountered some Boomers who just flat can't understand this generation. They see it as a lack of ambition, wondering why anyone would choose to not even try for a higher level position. Unfortunately this misunderstanding can lead to career derailment for Gen Xers and loss of great talent because of the

Boomers' inability to grasp Gen X values. Boomers will be much more successful leading Gen X if they remember that climbing the ladder is not the primary motivator for Gen X. In fact, according to Charlotte Shelton, a management consultant who teaches graduate courses at Rockhurst University's Helzberg School of Management in Kansas City, "The top three things they want in a job are

1. positive relationships with colleagues,
2. interesting work, and
3. continuous opportunities for learning."

For Gen X, "recognition scored very low, and power and prestige ranked dead last. Salary, a major preoccupation for Boomers, came in third from the bottom." Shelton adds: "It's interesting, because most employee-motivation efforts in companies are designed by Boomers, who tend to build the programs around what motivates them. But this generation is different."[5]

Of course there are some ambitious Gen Xers who are willing to play the Boomer game and climb the ladder as long as they are interested in the work, because they do want the top seats. They may want to be independent and put work-life balance above work on the priority list, but they are not stupid. Power is power, *and they do want the power.* Besides, once they have it, they can implement the Results-Only Work Environment, and then everyone will be happy—well, at least everyone in Gen X.

There is another little problem if you are a Boomer boss: *you* may be Gen X's number one career blocker, and they do not like career blockers. As a group, Gen X is becoming impatient (a true Gen X trait to start with) over its older siblings who are choosing to work longer than originally anticipated. Gen Xers were getting excited about taking the power, and now the Boomers are dashing their hopes.

> The "I'll work forever" attitude of the Baby Boomers is bringing movement up the career ladder to a complete standstill. It's like waiting for a table in a busy restaurant when the guests at the table you want have finished

their dessert and paid the bill but are busy chatting well beyond their 'allotted' time. The longer they stay, the more intense the glares and more uncomfortable everyone becomes."[6]

Organizations that want to keep their Gen X star performers shouldn't wait another moment. They will need new career path or development opportunities to keep them engaged while the Boomers drag out their exit plans. The last thing you want is to lose your next generation leaders because the current generation won't leave.

Okay, now back to the more "traditional" workplace and how to get and keep Gen X motivated to do the work that needs to be done. Here are a few key tips:

- Outline the role, but leave some flexibility for them to establish their unique characteristics and talents within the role.

- Establish expectations, including desired results and time-lines, and then become as hands-off as possible on how they get the results. As long as the results are delivered in a moral and ethical way, isn't the rest sort of semantics?

- In fact, encouraging their creativity and entrepreneurial spirit will go a long way in gaining a Gen X following.

- Allow Gen Xers to use technology in ways that Boomers have not. Gen X will probably want to work untethered to their desk and may not even need to have a desk or office space. While uncomfortable for most Boomers, considering the options here is a wise move. Remember, it's just a stepping stone into what Gen Y will want, so we may as well start adjusting now. After all, if the work gets done on time and with high quality, does it really matter where the work is done?

- Authoritarian management won't work with Gen Xers. They may take it for the moment as they smile and nod and tell the authoritarian manager, "Yes sir (or Yes ma'am), I understand," but they are most likely filing their mental ammunition to be fired at a later, more opportune moment.

- Gen Xers will accept constructive feedback as long as it is linked to results. To overcome their generational cynicism, it never hurts to have some data handy to back up the feedback. Leaders might think of themselves more as a hiking guide on a mountain terrain:

  1. Lead the way.

  2. Don't pretend you know the way if you've never been this way before. If you're going into uncharted territory, let your followers know. Gen X will rise to the challenge and help you find solutions, but they won't tolerate a leadership facade where you pretend you've done something before when you never have.

  3. Point out interesting areas for them to explore.

  4. Identify areas of danger and let them know the potential consequences of venturing into dangerous terrain.

  5. Whenever possible, take time to teach Gen Xers new skills and allow them to teach each other new skills.

  6. Give them time to explore and navigate on their own.

  7. Give them enough knowledge to make informed choices.

  8. Once you're comfortable with their skills and decision-making capabilities, point to the summit and turn them loose, but don't leave them on the mountain. Stay close enough to help if they slip or need some navigation advice along the way.

So you see, it is possible to lead Gen X. It just takes a little paradigm shifting to do it effectively. Ultimately, we all hope that the Boomers learn to lead and mentor Gen Xers and in turn, Gen Xers become effective leaders as their turn as "king of the mountain" approaches. What are the chances?

Notes

1.   Seuss, Dr. *Horton Hears a Who!* New York: Random House, 1954. Print.

2.   *Results-Only Work Environment (ROWE)*. Web. 24 July 2010. http://gorowe.com/.

3.   CultureRx Team. *Results-Only Work Environment (ROWE)*. Web. 01 Aug. 2010. http://gorowe.com/about/culturerx-team.

4.   Stauffer, David. "Motivating Across Generations." *Harvard Management Update.* Mar. 2003: 4. Print.

5.   Fisher, Anne. "How Best Companies to Work for Retain Gen Xers." *CNNMoney.com*. 17 Jan. 2006. Web. 24 July 2010. http://money.cnn.com/2006/01/17/news/companies/bestcos_ge nx/index.htm.

6.   Wolfe, Ira. "Are Baby Boomers Overstaying Their Welcome as Guests in the Workplace?" *Toolbox.com*. Toolbox for HR. Web. 24 July 2010. http://hr.toolbox.com/blogs/ira-wolfe/are-baby-boomers-overstaying-their-welcome-as-guests-in-the-workplace-35955.

Chapter 7 ────────────────

The Warfare Begins—Gen Y
Enters the Parade

> *I hear the train a comin'*
> *It's rolling round the bend.*
>
> — **Johnny Cash**
> **"Folsom Prison Blues"**[1]

Oh, yes. Here they come... Gen Y is entering the workforce, and boy, oh boy, is this going to be interesting. Just doing the research for this part of the book was a fascinating experience. We saw the excitement, the fear, and the controversy of this generation. As they enter the workforce portion of the generational parade, we see the Boomers and Gen Xers having optimistic hope, mild distaste, and the deep, long, truly-can't-stop belly laugh that comes from reading all the ideas Gen Y has about themselves. For instance, one blogger wrote the following: "Gen Y is here! We don't want to work hard, but we wants lots of vacation time and high salaries for no reason other then we think we deserve them!"[2] (We know the grammar is incorrect, but that's the way this Gen Yer wrote it, which is sort of a point all by itself.)

Now if you've never been an employer, you may not see the humor in that, but as small business owners and consultants who work with medium and large organizations, we find that to be very, very funny.

Now, let's see if we can paint an accurate picture of Gen Y.

Who are they?

Adjectives both good and bad abound for Gen Y, but the one we can't get away from is "coddled." They truly are used to getting what they want, when they want it. They are used to having their parents pay for it, and for many, graduating from college does not change that mindset at all. In fact, if they can't make enough to pay for their lifestyle, many Gen Yers just move back home. There's no argument that, as a group, Gen Y is smart, and they are using their smarts to get the lifestyle they want, even if it means Mom and Dad continue to pay for awhile.

They've also been labeled as "demanding," "disloyal," "impatient," "tattooed," "pierced," "techno-savvy," "pampered," "indulged," "can't focus on one thing at a time," and "high-maintenance feedback lovers." Some of this is no doubt true. After all, they are used to having the world at their fingertips via iPods and computers and using them all at once. They had cell phones before they hit puberty, and delayed gratification is not a concept they understand. Of course, that is because it wasn't taught, but let's not bring that up. It is, at least at times, not a pretty picture. But, in our research, we found one indisputable fact and that is that they are *young* and with youth comes some behaviors that will take care of themselves in due time.

On the other hand, Gen Y is bringing a lot of good to the world, at least potentially. It is the least prejudice of all the generations as far as we can tell. Hopefully that will be the case when it comes to age. Gen Yers hardly notice race other than to value the differences. They are very tolerant of the many types of lifestyles people choose to live, and they value ethnic differences. They are compassionate. They love working in teams and collaborating. In fact, they have figured out how to work in teams much more organically than the generations before them. While Boomers and Gen Xers fight for team leadership roles, Gen Y doesn't seem concerned. They are much more interested in being with their friends, doing interesting work, solving problems, and having fun. Yes, fun. This will be new for the workplace, because Boomers and Gen Xers have to schedule fun. It is not something they build into their lives naturally. Gen Y expects fun to be a part of their everyday work and life. In fact, the line between work and life is much fuzzier for Gen Y than what Boomers and Gen Xers are used to, but more on that later.

This generation also handles change better than the generations before it. Gen Yers are used to change coming almost at the speed of thought. While they may not be the most well-read, they are definitely the most well-informed generation. After all, they have their iPod, their iGoogle homepage, and their text-buddy grapevine to keep them totally informed at all times.

They have a consciousness for both socio-economic and health issues. They have their fingertips on everything from global economics to government policy, and of course, they have the monopoly on technology. And one very important note: Boomers and Gen Xers cannot—we repeat, *cannot*—compete in the technology arena. We are trying to learn, but let's face it, if we don't know how to do something, we call our Gen Y children, employees, or nieces and nephews. They walk over to our technology Rubik's Cube and line up the colors in no time at all and then smirk a little as if to say, "Loser."

Okay, maybe that's just how we feel and not what they're thinking but... "We're just sayin'...."

In addition to their technology expertise, Gen Yers are ambitious, but not in the same way as Boomers and Gen Xers. They have very high expectations for themselves, and they put pressure on themselves to do a good job. They are also an honest bunch—brutally honest at times. And—ugh!—they question everything: yes, everything from why they have to work at the office to why they have to start with grunt work and climb the ladder. They are not questioning everything to be annoying. They generally want to make it better, and questioning the status quo is their launching pad to making it better. They want to apply their technology expertise, their collaboration skills, and their ambition to making things better—and easier. Boomers and Gen Xers can complain and say they are lazy, but if they invent a robot to clean houses or take out the trash, you can bet everyone's going to use it. Besides, before complaining about their questioning, Boomers and Gen Xers should remember how they became the coddled, demanding, questioning, techno-obsessed troops that they are.

We Made Them that Way

That's right. We did this. Who is "we"? Well, both Boomers and Gen Xers have Gen Y children, so both are responsible. We have raised them primarily during times of easy access to finances, so they are not used to either holding back or cutting back. Whether it was out of guilt from the Boomers' workaholic lifestyle or over-compensating for our own independent lives, the Boomers and the Gen Xers have doted on Gen Y since the moment they were born. We've given them just about everything they could ask for and many things they would never have thought of if we hadn't presented it to them. We mean, how many Boomers and Gen Xers had hundreds of dollars spent on one of their birthday parties? Anyone? Oh, yes two of you, there in the back. Okay, now how many of us have spent hundreds of dollars on a birthday party for Gen Y?

Our point exactly.

Of course, that's all changing now. With the economic downturn, Gen Y has for the first time heard phrases like "We can't afford that right now" or "We don't have any more room on the credit card" or, big gasp, "We no longer use credit cards." Yes, it is a harsh reality for Gen Y and not so easy on the Boomers and Gen Xers either, but it's one of those sort of necessary corrections—like the stock market perhaps.

We've heard about China's "Little Emperors," referring to the only children in the People's Republic of China who are the product of the one-child policy that was implemented in that country, and it seems we may have made some little emperors of our own. We raised Gen Y to feel that they were special. And they are!

We have not withheld any form of media and struggled with figuring out what the appropriate limitations should be. We have enrolled them in so many things that we had to post spreadsheets on our refrigerators just to keep up with the family schedules.

In fact, according to many psychologists and parenting experts, we have treated Gen Y "more like partners than children as they were growing up." They cite families who allow a 6-year-old to choose the family car and pre-teens to decide where to go—or even whether to go—on vacation. They claim that "...the downside comes when kids grow up and realize they are not the center of the universe."[3]

While they may not be the true center of the universe, it does look like all eyes are turning to Gen Yers. Everyone wants to know how they learn, how they socialize, what they play, how they work, and especially how they buy. Gen Yers did not learn most of these patterns from their parents or older siblings; they are learning it together, making up their own rules. Both Boomers and Gen Xers are trying to figure out how to deal with and, more importantly, how to market to our little emperors.

It was so intriguing to the Boomer and Gen X parents to watch their Gen Y children begin to text incessantly while watching TV and playing on the computer that they didn't stop it. We weren't and still aren't sure if it was a good thing or a bad thing. We just continue to look with curiosity and think, "They certainly are 'good' multitaskers." At least they *do* a lot of multitasking. However, the research says multitasking makes us stupid. Okay, that's not exactly what it says, but research does prove that people lose IQ points when they multitask, and Gen Y is not excluded from this little phenomenon.

As an example, numerous studies have shown the sometimes-fatal danger of using cell phones and other electronic devices while driving, for example, and several states have now made that particular form of multitasking illegal. In the business world, where concerns about time management are perennial, warnings about workplace distractions spawned by a multitasking culture are on the rise. In 2005, the BBC reported on a research study, funded by Hewlett-Packard and conducted by the Institute of Psychiatry at the University of London, that found, "Workers distracted by e-mail and phone calls suffer a fall in IQ more than twice that found in marijuana smokers."[4] So, if we would all just focus on one thing at a time and smoke marijuana, we would still be smarter than the multitaskers. (It's just a joke Boomers. Don't get excited.)

So the Boomers and Gen Xers got together and created pampered, nurtured, questioning, fun-loving, feedback-giving, multitaskers who don't know the meaning of struggle and hardship. We've provided them enough technology to transform an undeveloped nation and have neglected to either practice or teach fiscal responsibility. Still, they are a tolerant group who care about community, the environment, animal rights, each other, and their parents. Could be worse....

Notes

1. Cash, Johnny. *Folsom Prison Blues*. Palobal, 1974. Vinyl recording.

2. Mitton, Kelly. "Generational Jousting." Web log post. *The Red Recruiter*. 23 Dec. 2009. Web. 24 July 2010. http://www.theredrecruiter.com/job-search/ generational-jousting.

3. "Psychology Across the Generations." *INSIGHT Magazine*. Dec. 2009. Web. 24 July 2010. http://insight-magazine.org/ 2009/headline/psychology-across-the-generations/.

4. Rosen, Christine. "The Myth of Multitasking." *The New Atlantis—A Journal of Technology & Society*. Spring 2008. Web. 24 July 2010. http://www.thenewatlantis.com/ publications/ the-myth-of-multitasking.

Chapter 8 ————————————
Being Led and Managed by Gen Y

Thirty pounds, ten years, one decent job, and one wife ago, you were at the top of your game. You were aging nicely, distinctive and refined, so they said. Just enough wisdom to be admired and still enough sex appeal to be desired; that was you. While you were putting your kids through college, life came crashing down around your comfortable shoes. Just as you made your last tuition payment, your investor was sent to prison.[1]

And now your new manager is a tattooed, text-addict, Gen Y, twenty-something. Look at the bright side. As Igor says in the 1974 movie *Young Frankenstein*,[2] it "Could be worse...could be raining."

So what can you expect from your Gen Y boss?

Well, let's be honest, we don't know a lot about Gen Y bosses yet because they are the youngest generation on the workforce playground. We do, however, have some examples to work with. There is Mark Zuckerberg, founder and CEO of Facebook. Working at this company is probably a good prelude to what we can expect, at least as long as the money holds out. We do have to remember that Facebook is still very young, and as its structure grows, it may look more like a traditional company, but here is what people are saying about working there at the moment:

- It is extremely fun to work with super bright people who have much better ideas than me. I get to talk with people who have similar interests and care about the Riya launch. Working 10–12-hour days seems like nothing and I could definitely stay there much longer if I didn't have to shower. Actually I hardly shower and we have a shower in the building. I think the idea of looking forward to work every day and missing it when I go home is a nice thought and more people should feel that at their companies.[3]

- It appears that if you start out where they need you (bottom of the ladder) and then "...within 3 to 6 months you move up the ladder to the position of your interest."[4]

- The trouble is that for a long time, Facebook had a reputation in Silicon Valley for being a place that, despite its white-hot user growth, still somehow had a hard time recruiting top talent to join the company. The gossip was Facebookers had to deal with an overly political workplace and amateurish management.

  Thanks to a professionalized recruiting team and a fancy new headquarters, there are some signs this reputation has changed. Headcount is now well over 800 employees and impressive hires are finally a regular occurrence.[5]

- One shared sentiment, though, is that Mark is a very demanding person to work for: if you screw up, one day you are in, the next day out, persona non grata.[6]

This last one is very interesting, but it isn't really anything new. Let's face it, we've had demanding CEOs from the dawn of time, and it isn't going to stop with Gen Y. As for the leadership being "amateurish," well, duh! The CEO started the company at 21. What else could he possibly be? Now the working 10 to 12 hours and not wanting to leave, that we really must learn more about.

Career coaches have said it for years and apparently it's true. Happiness in a career is most closely tied to your *interests*. So, when Facebook allows employees to try on different "roles," it helps them gravitate toward their area of interest. This is breakthrough stuff. Pay attention older generations. One Gen Yer wrote a great article (online of course) about how he thinks they'll change the workforce. Now we all know that saying you'll do it and doing it are two very different things, but we think his article is worth reading, so we've printed it here with permission:

10 Ways Generation Y
Will Change the Workplace

by Ryan Healey
Co-Founder and COO of Brazen Careerist
(www.BrazenCareerist.com)

There's no doubt that Generation Y will fundamentally change corporate America. It's already started. Managing Gen Y is the hot topic among consultants, Human Resource executives, and talent management professionals. For a Gen Yer like me, this is great news.

We have a voice, and we have the ear of the decision makers. Not bad for a group of lazy, entitled, twenty-somethings. We've learned the importance of balancing work and life from our over-worked parents, and we've watched our older siblings and cousins struggle with their boomer bosses who refuse to retire. Now we're primed to change the workplace for the better. Here's how we'll do it.

1. **We'll hold only productive meetings.** Meetings are important, sometimes. A good meeting will pull everyone to the same page while motivating them to get the work done. It's rare when that should take more than 30 minutes. Efficiency is the name of the game with Gen Y. We know that a drawn-out meeting really means "We have no idea what we're doing," and these time suckers actually halt productivity and stifle creativity, the qualities that they were supposed to encourage. As soon as Gen Y is running the show, watch wasted meeting time drop dramatically.

2. **We'll shorten the work day.** The work day is eight hours. Or so they say. A real work day for most of us, if you include the commute, lunch, breaks, and maybe dinner, is at least 10 hours. But how many hours of the day are actually spent doing real work? I would guess about half. To truly balance work and life, you cannot mess around and waste time at the office. Gen Y knows this. We're productivity machines; we will figure out

how to get as much done in six to seven hours as the average boomer does with his eight.

3. **We'll bring back the administrative assistants.** Back in the day, nearly everyone had a secretary. These days, you have to be a CEO or high-level executive for a Fortune 500 company to have an assistant. Sure, this saves the company a ton, but Generation Y won't stand for it much longer. We recognize the value of time. Two extra hours per day not filing papers and mailing checks adds up to over 500 extra hours per year that we can spend with family and friends. Even if it comes out of our own pocket, Gen Y will cough up the extra dough to get a part-time or virtual assistant.

4. **We'll redefine retirement.** Retirement is dead. It's dead for a number of reasons, including the issues with social security and middle class America's inability to save any money. But Gen Y will figure out how to save money to retire—we're already demanding 401(k)s and excellent benefits. However, we will re-invent retirement by taking multiple mini-retirements instead of calling it quits a few years before its time to croak. Maybe in our late twenties we'll take a few months just to travel the world. Then, as we approach parenthood and our kids grow up, we'll take a year off to enjoy time with our family. Then we'll return to work, refreshed and ready to go. When we hit 65, it will be the new 45 and we'll have a solid 15 to 20 years left before we take our final, very brief, mini-retirement.

5. **We'll find real mentors.** Gen Y is obsessed with career development. We understand the importance of great mentors and we seek them out. The problem is that many older workers weren't effectively mentored and they don't always know how to mentor Gen Y. When it's Gen Y's turn to be senior mentors, we'll know how. As we seek mentors now, we'll learn what works and what doesn't. And from the time we enter the workforce until the time we're senior employees, the smartest Gen Yers will figure out how to mentor up. We will teach our older co-workers about new technologies and the power of

online communities, and they will respond kindly by guiding us through the insane office politics that exist everywhere.

6. **We'll restore respect to the HR Department.** Ten years ago, human resources got no respect. Today, companies are just beginning to see the importance. Gen Y recognizes that people make the company successful. Maybe it's not tangible and maybe it's not easy to see the direct ROI on keeping people happy, but happy people create successful organizations. All you need to do is take a look at Goggle, the company that's quickly taking over the world, to see that happy people are successful people and successful people make a lot of money for themselves and for the company. HR is not a cost center, it's vital to the bottom line.

7. **We'll promote based on emotional intelligence.** For some reason, companies assume that when you pay your dues and you know the business, you can be a manager. They're wrong. The truth is that seniority does not make a good manager. People skills make a good manager. By the time Gen Y is running the world, we will be smart enough to promote people to managers because they can manage, not because they've worked for ten years. For managers, personal work must come a distant second to developing employees both personally and professionally. If you can't help others, you don't deserve a promotion to manager and you will be left behind.

8. **We'll continue to value what our parents have to offer.** Sure, Gen Xers can laugh about it now, but Gen Yers respect our parents, and our parents are interested in every part of our lives, even when we're 30. Don't be surprised to see Gen Y employees giving their parents a tour of the office and calling up mom and dad for a little advice on their lunch break. It's not about being babied or refusing to grow up, it's about a level of mutual respect that Gen Y has for our parents and our parents have for us. My mother is coming to visit in a couple of weeks, and guess what our plan for the day is? A tour of the office and a couple hours of work for each of us before we go out and do the tourist thing.

9. **We'll enjoy higher starting salaries.** Sure, Gen Y is interested in volunteering, putting a halt to global warming and all that other good stuff, but we're not our idealist parents. We watched our parents get laid off and we know that companies look out for themselves, so we do the same. Gen Yers will gladly accept a higher starting salary than promises of raises and promotions that we may never see. Additionally, all we have to do is go to Payscale.com or some other site to find out what the average starting salary is. Then we will ask for more, and we'll probably get it, because we know we can get it elsewhere if your company won't give it to us.

10. **We'll re-invent the performance review.** Semi-annual or annual performance reviews do not work. Gen Y wants constant feedback. If we're only at a company for two years, we cannot wait for our one-year review to find out how we're doing. Gen Y will invent the on-the-spot performance review. The smartest companies will train their managers in giving frequent feedback, and the companies that don't will get a quick reality check when their Gen Y employees demand them. Spot reviews lead to consistent improvement, and consistent improvement is what truly matters to Generation Y.[7]

We love this! Of course they are sort of saying that we

1. hold unproductive meetings;
2. create long work days;
3. nix our administrative assistants;
4. designed a faulty retirement process;
5. use and are ineffective mentors;
6. disrespect the HR Department;
7. promote based on skill rather than management ability;
8. don't value our parents;
9. prefer low starting salaries;
10. don't provide adequate feedback.

Okay, we'll try not to be offended, especially if some of it rings a little true. But, hey, let's look at this another way: when Gen Y leads, they can get to work fixing all of these problems we created. Yes, it will be hard, and we have no idea how they are going to fund these changes, but we won't have to worry about it. Why? Because they will be in charge, and since we don't really know how to be good mentors, they probably won't ask us. But we will be available in case they do. We'll be happy to work together to solve these workplace problems while we sit in very productive meetings with our high salaries and administrative assistants to take the notes. We mean, we're going to want in on all of these perks. It would be workplace inequality to leave the Boomers and Gen Xers out of the workplace changes. Making these changes looks like a lot of work for the HR Department, but we're sure they won't mind because of the new level of respect they will hold. However, if they do mind, we're sure they'll let you know with the new constant feedback processes Gen Y puts in place. On the other hand, if it's before 9:00 a.m. or after 4:00 p.m., they probably won't let you know because Gen Y isn't into long work hours. We love it! Where do we sign up?

Yes, we're having a little fun at the expense of Gen Y, but we don't mean any harm. Seriously, Gen Y has some great ideas and with their highly educated, techno-savvy masses, we know that they are going to bring a lot of seriously fun and exciting changes to the workforce. Who knows, we may like Gen Y's ideas so much that we may continue to (we mean start to) finance them.

Notes

1.   Clements, Priscilla. "Babyboomers—We're Broke. We Lost Our Jobs. We Lost Our Houses. Now We're Loosing Our Hair!" *Associated Content*. 17 Dec. 2009. Web. 24 July 2010. http://www.associatedcontent.com/article/2501401/ babyboomers_were_broke_we_lost_our.html.

2.   *Young Frankenstein*. Dir. Mel Brooks. Perf. Gene Wilder and Peter Boyle. Gruskoff/Venture Films, 1974. DVD.

3.   Kagan, Noah. "Life at Facebook, 3 Weeks at a Startup." *Noah Kagan's Okdork.com*. 1 Dec. 2005. Web. 24 July 2010. http://okdork.com/2005/12/01/life-at-facebook-3-weeks-at-a-startup/.

4.   Carlson, Nicholas. "Will Working at Facebook Blow like Google Customer Service? No." *Valleywag—Gawker*. 4 Mar. 2008. Web. 24 July 2010. http://valleywag.gawker.com/ 363457/ will-working-at-facebook-blow-like-google-customer-service-no.

5.   Miller, Alaska, and Nicholas Carlson. "What Is It Like Working at Facebook?" *Business Insider, Inc.* 14 Dec. 2009. Web. 24 July 2010. http://www.businessinsider.com/what-is-it-like-working-at-facebook-2009-12.

6.   Carlson, Nicholas. "Why Top Execs Keep Quitting Facebook." *Business Insider*. 13 Mar. 2009. Web. 24 July 2010. http://www.businessinsider.com/why-so-many-top-execs-keep-quitting-facebook-2009-3.

7.   Healy, Ryan. "Crystal Ball: 10 Ways Generation Y Will Change the Workplace | Brazen Careerist." *Brazen Careerist*. 23 May 2008. Web. 24 July 2010. http://www.brazencareerist.com/ 2008/05/23/crystal-ball-10-ways-generation-y-will-change-the-workplace/.

Chapter 9 ——————————
Leading and Managing Gen Y

Don Tapscott in *Grown Up Digital* said, "I think we're seeing the early signs of a major collision between the freewheeling Net Generation (Gen Y) and the traditional boomer employers. It's not necessarily a clash between Net Geners and Boomers as human beings. It's a clash between two ideas of how work should work."[1]

We agree that there is a clash coming, and coming soon: Boomers think Gen Y needs to face reality; Gen Y thinks the Boomers and the Gen Xers need to "chill"; and the Gen Xers don't care.

Managing Gen Y may seem like a daunting task, but remember that the landscape is changing in more ways than one. In fact, it will be quite a wake-up call for Gen Yers as they face over 20 percent unemployment at entry level. This precipitates a fiercely competitive job climate that will benefit employers and serve up the most ambitious, multitasking, hard-working new recruits they have seen in decades. Put that together with the slow economy, and you have a hiring leader's dream. Unfortunately for employers, we are not seeing this great employer-friendly climate just yet, and that is because we are on the front end of the bell curve when it comes to Gen Y.

So Boomers and Gen Xers will have to learn how to manage Gen Yers as they are and, at the same time, provide some gentle but consistent guidance so that we can all round the corner together into the new workplace environment. After all, taking a hard right curve to get to the "new" workplace environment is not the right answer. If we trash our current processes and structures and move to the environment Gen Y wants, it will be too much change at once, and it disregards all the hard work, foundation, and structure that the Boomers and Gen Xers have put into place.

It brings to mind the old phrase, "Don't throw out the baby with the bath water."

> *Each generation goes further than the generation preceding it because it stands on the shoulders of that generation. You will have opportunities beyond anything we've ever known.*
>
> **— Ronald Reagan**

As a whole, we must continue to move forward, adjusting both to the swift advancements in technology and globalization as well as the unique characteristics of our incoming workforce. And there is really no argument that this is going to be a challenge.

When working with coaching clients, Hagemann often has them envision their ideal work life, project outcome, presentation, or other important scenario as a beginning process to move toward an ultimate goal. So we did a sort of "collective visioning" by pulling together everything we could find on the "ideal" work scenario for Gen Y. We wanted to answer the question, what does Gen Y want? So we went looking for the answer, and here's what we found…. Drum roll please.

They want it all! That's what they want. Don't look so surprised. Isn't that what the Boomers and the Gen Xers want? It doesn't mean we're going to get it, but we do all *want it,* now don't we? Specifically, though, Gen Y's list of wants can seem a bit daunting to any manager or employer.

Here are some of the common themes in Gen Yers' long list of wants:

- to work for an employer who is honest, up-to-date, speedy, and green
- to be totally connected and at the same time totally untethered
- to be able to access their social networks, online games, etc., at work
- to be able to work on things they are passionate about
- to have full benefits and a lot of vacation
- to have customizable roles and responsibilities
- to have customizable schedule options such as part-time, flextime, temporary project-based work, job sharing, seasonal employment, shift work, and of course, telecommuting
- to have great technology with lots of techno paraphernalia and to have their employer pay for it
- to collaborate, solve problems, and work on interesting things
- to receive lots of feedback—constant feedback
- to receive personal attention from their boss
- to work on interesting and challenging work (read: "they do not want to start with grunt work and climb the ladder to higher levels")
- to be on a team, but they do *not* want to lead a team, department, or business unit

To wrap it all up in a neat little package, we find that they really don't *want* to be job hoppers, but they are because today's workplace doesn't "fit" Gen Yers very well, so they keep looking for that right fit.

So, we've been wondering who is going to do the work that requires independence and managing others: you know, the work that isn't fun such as the leadership role (target on back with arrows sticking out of the target) or interesting such as the boring jobs that are simply maintenance or service oriented. Who's going to pick up the trash in the garbage trucks or handle mountains of monotonous accounting spreadsheets? It has to be done, but Gen Yers say they aren't going to do it. Boomers? Gen Xers? Anyone?

No one? Well, we can all see the problem. There is a clash coming, but when we sort through all the naiveté and "dream job" wishes, we can narrow the clash down to a few key areas.

Technology

Gen Yers want unlimited access to high-speed technology, and they also want access to social networking such as Facebook and instant messaging chats with their friend on work time. Gen Yers are most comfortable when they are engaged simultaneously in multiple activities such as listening to music, texting, and writing, but Boomer and even Gen Xer employers are not likely to understand or embrace paying for social time. Regardless, employers are going to have to deal with this issue soon, so creating processes, guidelines, and policies should probably start now if not already in progress.

What's the right answer on how to deal with all this? No one knows for sure. This is one of those areas where we are just going to have to try some things, realizing that we are going to make mistakes and be willing to change when we do. However, unless your organization is under tight security such as the defense industry, it may be best to embrace the use of technology and social networking at work versus fighting it. It should be noted that there are potential security risks with allowing social networking at work. It allows an opening for viruses and spyware. It also presents a legal risk as employees can download intellectual property and put the company at risk for a lawsuit. According to David Kelleher, a communications and research analyst at GFI, the companies who are in the middle ground when it comes to security typically have processes that

> monitor all Web activity and control it on a per-user basis when social networking sites can be accessed at the office. Administrators can use Web monitoring software to block access during most of the day except during the staff lunch break or before and after normal office hours. The same software can be used to ensure that any files downloaded or links accessed online are checked in real time for exploits, malware, and viruses.[2]

It is work after all. It costs organizations millions to extract viruses and spyware, and we live in a lawsuit happy world, so providing some sort of process seems logical, but be aware that Gen Y may find the "middle ground" a bit stifling. Here is what a sample social networking and social media policy for this tactic might look like:

1. Include in your personal blogs clear disclaimers that the views expressed by the author in the blog are the author's alone and do not represent the views of the company. Be clear and write in first person. Make your writing clear that you are speaking for yourself and not on behalf of the company.

2. Ensure that information published on your blog(s) complies with the company's confidentiality and disclosure of proprietary data policies. This also applies to comments posted on other blogs, forums, and social networking sites.

3. Be respectful to the company, other employees, customers, partners, and competitors.

4. Do not allow social media activities to interfere with work commitments. Refer to IT resource usage policies.

5. Be aware that your actions captured via images, posts, or comments can reflect that of the company.

6. Do not reference or site company clients, partners, or customers without their express consent. In all cases, do not publish any information regarding a client during the engagement.

7. Respect copyright laws, and reference or cite sources appropriately. Plagiarism applies online as well.

8. Do not use company logos and trademarks without written consent.[3]

The truth is that if employers do a good job of hiring and Gen Yers do a good job of choosing their work, they will be so engaged in the work that time spent on activities outside of work will be minimal. They'll stay focused, not because they have to, but because they like the work.

Their Need for Feedback

Another potential for cosmic clash is Gen Y's need for feedback. The Boomers have put systems in place for annual, bi-annual, or quarterly performance feedback. These are great systems with expensive technology and years and years of work of honing down the process to a science. The Gen Xers have grudgingly submitted to this painful scheduled experience, but now Gen Yers are entering the scene and they don't want the scheduled feedback; instead, they want constant feedback. By constant, we mean constant. One of Hagemann's Gen Y children brought home straight As at Christmas and by January 20th said she was no longer a straight A student because she had a B in Communication Arts. Hagemann explained to her daughter that she was technically still considered an A student until her next report card came out and that she had plenty of time to bring her grade back up to an A. Her daughter was still very disappointed in herself, checking her grades constantly until she was back in A status. Notice it was not Hagemann (Gen X mom) insisting on the A status. It was the Gen Y daughter. The same behavior can be expected from Gen Yers at work. Boomers and Gen Xers can forget about the annual performance review. If they only give Gen Yers feedback once per year, they won't be there to give feedback to.

Remember, Gen Yers live in real time. They want their feedback that way, their technology that way, and who knows what else. They will not only ask their Boomer and Gen X boss for feedback, but they will also ask their peers and, yes, their parents. In fact, "a large proportion of Ys (42% of women and 30% of men) report that they talk to their parents **every day**."[4]

On this front, we're sure Boomers and Gen Xers will be able to eventually adjust. It may feel a little high maintenance at first, but in the long run, it should put an end forever to the surprise "we're going to let you go" discussion, because with constant feedback, employees should know exactly where they stand. Well, maybe that's a little overly optimistic. Still, we think it will be a good thing in the long run. There is one more issue about constant feedback: Gen Yers not only want to receive it, but they also want to give it.

Making Their Voice Heard

Gen Yers love to give feedback as much as they love to receive it. They will want to give feedback in real time. And, they are brutally honest, which neither the Boomers or Gen Xers are likely to appreciate. Gen Y is going to question all of our established processes all of the time. For example, workplace attire: Boomers and Gen X were fine with going to business casual, but Gen Y is really more along the lines of "very casual" vs. "business casual." Gen Yers are also significantly more pierced and tattooed than the majority of their older generational predecessors.

"Gen Y is also much less likely to respond to the traditional command-and-control type of management still popular in much of today's workforce," says Jordan Kaplan, an associate managerial science professor at Long Island University—Brooklyn in New York. "They've grown up questioning their parents, and now they're questioning their employers. They don't know how to shut up, which is great, but that's aggravating to the 50-year-old manager who says, 'Do it and do it now.'" [5]

Case in point: David L. Larson, professor and chair of the department of plastic surgery at the Medical College of Wisconsin (Milwaukee), and his peers found themselves increasingly troubled by the behavior and perceived attitudes of residents. "Some of us would tell a resident to do something, and he or she would question it or simply not do it," says Larson. "We sensed different values. Some residents bluntly told their directors to chill out—that they worked too hard." [6]

It isn't that Gen Yers are trying to be disrespectful. We have to remember that. They have grown up with their input being valued, so why should that change just because they are now employed? It may be irritating for Boomers and Gen Xers, but learning to accept and give feedback is ultimately a good thing all the way around. The only downside we can think of is if employers tried to make constant changes based on feedback. When a leader receives feedback, it is the patterns that should be focused on, not the individual comments, because it's impossible to make everyone happy. So leaders shouldn't try to make all their employees happy, even if they are the squeaky wheel. In the end, it is the valuing of each person's opinion that is good for morale.

Another way Gen Yers will make their voices heard is in the company's marketing. If the company markets in a way that Gen Yers feel is dishonest, expect them to be very vocal about it. Since just about everything ends up on the Internet these days, don't expect to "spin" the message or your brand. The Internet really is the no-spin zone, because the truth is generally revealed and the only problem is figuring out which post is the truth. In fact, companies will need to listen to Gen Yers on this front, because they will leave if they feel that the organization is lacking integrity in its marketing. Yes, it may be a little hypocritical for this music-lifting generation, but prepare yourself none-the-less.

Learning and Development

Learning and development have become common workplace terms with many organizations devoting full-time staff and entire departments and sometimes incorporating entire corporate universities for the structured learning and development of their employees. This is great for Gen Yers because they will show up, even in the interview, wanting to know how the company will invest in their personal learning and development. Providing these opportunities will be a core component of employing Gen Y.

For employers who do not have a learning and development mindset, it's time to start. It doesn't have to be a budget-buster. Mentoring programs can be implemented very cost-effectively as can Leaders as Teachers programs. In both of these development opportunities, you are using existing talent to grow and develop new talent. We've included more learning and development options in Chapter 15.

May we suggest a few areas where these learning and development programs may want to focus? Well, since you asked.... If it were our company, we would build programs that help Gen Y gain abilities in extended times of focused concentration on a person, topic, or problem. This is a great area for mentors and current leaders to begin growing this young talent. And Gen Yers will respond favorably to the personal attention.

Another area is around structure and time on the "clock." All of their childhood, scheduled sporting events gave Gen Yers a lot of structure, and they will expect to have structure in the workplace, too. However, just like their sporting events, they expect to show up, complete a task or solve a problem, and then go home or elsewhere. They do not see any point in hanging around because the 5 o'clock whistle hasn't blown yet. (Does anyone still blow a 5 o'clock whistle?) Helping Gen Y understand the current structure and create their own where needed will be a great way to help them develop.

Gen Yers like a challenge, so help them understand the bureaucracy so that they can jump into areas of opportunity and show off their capabilities. They love problem-based learning, so once they understand which sacred cows should be kicked and which ones just aren't worth it, turn them loose on some of your stickiest problems. Let them work in small teams and give them space to solve the problem. We think you'll be surprised at what they can do.

A few other areas we might suggest for the development of Gen Y include

- communication and self-awareness;
- self-management;
- financial acumen;
- critical thinking and problem solving; and
- writing skills.

Mentoring is a great way to develop Gen Y, and since they appreciate structure and stability, it will help to create a formal process, with set meetings and a more authoritative attitude on the mentor's part. [7]

In addition to developing Gen Yers, remember to cut them a little slack when they first enter the workforce, especially if they've had had to, ah-hum, "start at the bottom." It's hard on them. They weren't expecting this. You can see it in this Gen Y quote:

> Collectively, my generation has an abundance of pride, and it takes a great deal of discouragement and failed attempts for one to admit that they graduated and now work at Macy's or Olive Garden. Actually, it wasn't until graduates couldn't financially survive that they surrendered to working as a hostess after dedicating so much time and effort throughout college.

> Perhaps we, the Millennial Generation, felt too entitled to a decent job with benefits upon graduation and that's why it is so hard to settle for less. Perhaps the realization that our dream jobs are not even open to applicants is what brought on the fear and anxiety. That feeling of entitlement quickly vanished as the job market began to crash, and more graduates prepared themselves to fail

rather than succeed in finding this so called "deserved" job.[8]

So reality hits even the most optimistic at some point, just like it did and is still doing for the Boomers and Gen Xers. The only difference between us and Gen Y is that when reality hits, it will feel more familiar to us.

It's true that Gen Y is asking for a lot when it comes to work and work-life balance. Even more frightening is that if the Boomer and Gen Xer bosses are not giving it to them, they may request a new boss. After all, they had their parents request a new teacher when the one they had wasn't meeting their needs. They changed university professors when the teaching wasn't what they wanted or expected. Why should they have to endure a boss who isn't working for them? It could happen, so the Boomer and Gen Xer bosses shouldn't be surprised. However, if it's a pattern, then they may want to do a little growth and development of their own.

Regardless of the daunting list of wants, it is possible to create an environment that is attractive to this generation. Now, we haven't worked there personally, but we think Google may have it figured out. Here's what they offer according to their web site (www.google.com):

Benefits

The goal is to strip away everything that gets in our employees' way. We provide a standard package of fringe benefits, but on top of that are first-class dining facilities, gyms, laundry rooms, massage rooms, haircuts, car-washes, dry cleaning, commuting buses—just about anything a hardworking employee might want. Let's face it: programmers want to program, they don't want to do their laundry. So we make it easy for them to do both.

— **Eric Schmidt, CEO Google**

Google's founders often state that the company is not serious about anything but search. They built a company around the idea that work should be challenging and the challenge should be fun. To that end, Google's culture is unlike any in corporate America, and it's not because of the whimsical lava lamps and large rubber balls, or the fact that one of the company's chefs used to cook for the Grateful Dead. In the same way Google puts users first when it comes to online services, Google puts employees first when it comes to daily life in its offices.

> **Benefits Philosophy:** We strive to be innovative and unique in all services we provide both to customers and employees, including our benefits and perks offerings. We realize and celebrate that our employees have diverse needs, and that this diversity requires flexible and individually directed support. Our priority is to offer a customizable program that can be tailored to the specific needs of each individual, whether they enjoy ice climbing in Alaska, want to retire by age 40, or plan to adopt three children.

Health and Wellness

Medical Insurance: Three Carriers

Carriers for California:
- Blue Shield: PPO (Preferred Provider Organization) or HMO (Health Maintenance Organization)
- CIGNA: PPO or EPP (Exclusive Provider Medical Benefits)
- Kaiser

Carriers for Other States:
- Blue Shield: PPO (Preferred Provider Organization) or OOA (Out of Area)
- CIGNA: PPO or EPP (Exclusive Provider Medical Benefits)

Dental Insurance
Comprehensive coverage through Delta Dental

Vision Insurance
Exams, contacts, lenses and frames all generously covered

Flex Spending Account Plan
Includes Health Spending Account, Dependent Care Account and Qualified Transportation Benefit

EAP—Employee Assistance Program
Services for employees and their dependents include free short-term counseling, legal consultations, financial counseling, child care referrals and pet care referrals

Life and AD&D Insurance
Automatic coverage at two times annual salary

Voluntary Life Insurance
Option to purchase additional life insurance

Short-Term and Long-Term Disability
Short-Term Disability Insurance coverage provided at approximately 100% of normal of salary. Long-Term Disability coverage provided at 66⅔% of salary once Short-Term Disability is exhausted

Business Travel Accident Insurance
Automatic coverage at two times annual salary

Retirement and Savings

Google 401(k) Plan
Employees may contribute up to 60% and receive a Google match of up to the greater of (a) 100% of your contribution up to $2,500 or (b) 50% of your contribution per year with no vesting schedule! We offer a variety of investment options to choose from, through Vanguard, our 401(k) Plan Administrator. To help you with those tough investment decisions, employees can access Financial Engines to receive personalized investment advice.

529 College Savings Plan
This plan provides employees with a way to save money for post-secondary education

Time away

Vacation
- 1st year: 15 days
- 4th year: 20 days
- 6th year: 25 days

Holidays
12 paid holidays (sick days taken as necessary)

Maternity Benefits
Up to 18 weeks off at approximately 100% pay

Parental Leave (for non-primary caregivers)
Up to 7 weeks off at approximately 100% pay

Take-Out Benefit
To help make things easier, new moms and dads are able to expense up to $500 for take-out meals during the first three months that they are home with their new baby

Benefits ... Beyond the Basics

Tuition Reimbursement
We'll help you pursue further education that's relevant to what you do. You must receive grades of "B" or better. Why a "B" or better? Because we said so. Tuition reimbursement is $12,000 per calendar year

Employee Referral Program
Good people know other good people. Our best employees have been hired through referrals. Google encourages you to recommend candidates for opportunities here and will award you a bonus if your referral accepts our offer and remains employed for at least 60 days

Back-Up Child Care
As a California employee, when your regularly scheduled child care falls through, Google will provide you with five free days of child care per year through Children's Creative Learning Center (CCLC); 13 Bay Area locations serving ages 6 weeks to 12 years

Gift Matching Program

Google matches contributions of up to $3,000 per year from eligible employees to non-profit organizations. Bolstering employee contributions to worthy causes with matching gifts doesn't just mean helping hundreds of organizations, both locally and globally; it's also a tangible expression. We want Googlers to get involved—and the company is right behind you.

Adoption Assistance

Google assists our employees by offering financial assistance in the adoption of a child. We'll reimburse you up to $5,000 to use towards legal expenses, adoption agencies or other adoption professional fees. Parental leave and take-out benefit also apply

Benefits ... Way Beyond the Basics

Food

Hungry? Check out our free lunch and dinner—our gourmet chefs create a wide variety of healthy and delicious meals every day. Got the munchies? Google also offers snacks to help satisfy you in between meals

On-Site Doctor

At Google headquarters in Mountain View, California, you have the convenience of seeing a doctor on-site

Shuttle Service

Google is pleased to provide its Mountain View employees with free shuttles to several San Francisco, East Bay and South Bay locations

Financial Planning Classes

Google provides objective and conflict-free financial education classes. The courses are comprehensive and cover a variety of financial topics

Other On-Site Services

At Google headquarters in Mountain View, there's on-site oil change, car wash, dry cleaning, massage therapy, gym, hair stylist, fitness classes and bike repair

Other Great Benefits

Halloween and holiday party, health fair, credit union, sauna, roller hockey, outdoor volleyball court, discounts for products and local attractions."[9]

And they didn't stop there! Google goes for the heart of their employees. Here are their **Top 10 Reasons to Work at Google:**

1. **Lend a helping hand.** With millions of visitors every month, Google has become an essential part of everyday life—like a good friend—connecting people with the information they need to live great lives.

2. **Life is beautiful.** Being a part of something that matters and working on products in which you can believe is remarkably fulfilling.

3. **Appreciation is the best motivation**, so we've created a fun and inspiring workspace you'll be glad to be a part of, including on-site doctor and dentist; massage and yoga; professional development opportunities; shoreline running trails; and plenty of snacks to get you through the day.

4. **Work and play are not mutually exclusive.** It is possible to code and pass the puck at the same time.

5. **We love our employees, and we want them to know it.** Google offers a variety of benefits, including a choice of medical programs, company-matched 401(k), stock options, maternity and paternity leave, and much more.

6. **Innovation is our bloodline.** Even the best technology can be improved. We see endless opportunity to create even more relevant, more useful, and faster products for our users. Google is the technology leader in organizing the world's information.

7. **Good company everywhere you look.** Googlers range from former neurosurgeons, CEOs, and U.S. puzzle champions to alligator wrestlers and Marines. No matter what their backgrounds, Googlers make for interesting cube mates.

8. **Uniting the world, one user at a time.** People in every country and every language use our products. As such we think, act, and work globally—just our little contribution to making the world a better place.

9. **Boldly go where no one has gone before.** There are hundreds of challenges yet to solve. Your creative ideas matter here and are worth exploring. You'll have the opportunity to develop innovative new products that millions of people will find useful.

10. **There is such a thing as a free lunch after all.** In fact we have them every day: healthy, yummy, and made with love. [10]

Yes, it's a jaw-dropping list and not just appealing to Gen Y. It looks pretty good to Boomers and Gen Xers, too. In fact, Google, if you're looking for some *seasoned* talent, give us a call. We'll be waiting by the phone.

For those companies less fortunate than Google, relax. Remember the parade: Gen Y is continually filing into the workplace parade, and their numbers are massive. They are going to need more jobs than there are jobs available, so if you can't compete with Google, don't worry. Gen Y will also eventually be celebrating the day their friends get a job—any job.

Notes

1.   Tapscott, Don. *Grown Up Digital: How the Net Generation Is Changing Your World*. New York: McGraw-Hill, 2009. Print. p. 153.

2.   Kelleher, David. "Social Networking at Work: Fear Not Facebook, MySpace?" *ITworld*. ITworld's Daily Newsletter, 23 Feb. 2009. Web. 24 July 2010. http://www.itworld. com/internet/ 63062/social-networking-work-fear-not-facebook-myspace?page=0,2.

3.   Hoang, Daniel. "Sample Social Networking Policy." *TBusinessEdge.com*. 6 Mar. 2009. Web. 24 July 2010. http://www.itbusinessedge.com/cm/docs/DOC-1257.

4.   Hewlett, Sylvia, Laura Sherbin, and Karen Sumberg. "How Gen Y and Boomers Will Reshape Your Agenda." *Harvard Business Review*. 1 July 2009. Web. 24 July 2010. http://hbr.org/product/ how-gen-y-and-boomers-will-reshape-your-agenda/an/R0907G-PDF-ENG.

5.   Armour, Stephanie. "Generation Y: They've Arrived at Work with a New Attitude." *USATODAY*. 11 Nov. 2005. Web. 24 July 2010. http://www.usatoday.com/money/ workplace/2005-11-06-gen-y_x.htm.

6.   Stauffer, David. "Motivating Across Generations." *Harvard Management Update* (Mar. 2003): 4. Print.

7.   Thielfoldt, Diane, and Devon Scheef. "Generation X and The Millennials: What You Need to Know About Mentoring the New Generations." *American Bar Association—Defending Liberty, Pursuing Justice*. Law Practice Today, Aug. 2004. Web. 24 July 2010. http://www.abanet.org/lpm/lpt/articles/ mgt08044.html.

8. "No Goals in 2010." Weblog post. *Oilandgarlic's Blog*. 23 Dec. 2009. Web. http://oilandgarlic.wordpress.com/ 2009/ 12/23/no-goals-in-2010/.

9. "Benefits—U.S. Jobs." *Google*. Web. 24 July 2010. http:// www.google.com/jobs/lifeatgoogle/benefits/#ta.

10. "Top Ten Reasons to Work at—U.S. Jobs." *Google*. Web. 24 July 2010. http://www.google.com/jobs/lifeatgoogle/ toptenreasons/.

Chapter 10 ────────────────
What does it all mean?

So many things are positive about Gen Yers that we could be fooled into thinking that we should just give them the keys, but, not so.... They are young, and young people make "young people's mistakes." They underestimate the time and money it will take to get things done, just like we did. They will make mistakes in managing and leading others that will be costly and sometimes crushing. They'll underestimate their lack of respect for intellectual property and be shocked when they make mistakes that cause their employer to hire a team of lawyers that will have to work for years to defend their "innocent sharing" of intellectual property. They need the wisdom and the structure that Boomers and Gen Xers bring to the workplace. They need opportunity, development, feedback, and growth, and they need guidance. They will probably also have to do some of the menial work that none of us wanted to do but most of us had to do. And why not? Why should they miss out on such excellent character-building opportunities?

Of course they are innovative, so maybe if we give them some room, they can figure out how to get the menial work done without actually doing it via robotics, electronics, and other creative solutions. We hope so, but the quickly approaching storm is still the Boomer's exiting, not Gen Y coming.

Due to generational differences, the Boomers have not been good about sharing their knowledge and experience, and Gen X has not been good about tapping into it. Currently, 65 percent of all national leaders are Boomers. The Boomers "retain much of the experiential, technical, institutional and political knowledge in the workplace. They have the industry connections, networks, and inside scoop to get things done. They have experienced successes and learned from their failures. They are community builders and can galvanize a force of their own at the drop of a hat. And they have vision. Those are the characteristics that Gen Xers need to learn in order to assume the leadership mantle in the future."[1]

Not one of the generations has it all figured out. Well, maybe Gen Yers still think that, but they won't for long. Paul Watzlawick once said, "The belief that one's own view of reality is the only reality is the most dangerous of all delusions." Hopefully each generational group realizes that we can learn from each other and that our collective wisdom should bring about a truly better workplace for everyone.

In William Bridges's work around transitions, he states that a change is when something stops and then something else begins. But a transition is something that happens over time. It usually has an ending, a neutral zone, and then a new beginning. Bridges says that it is in the neutral zone where there is chaos. It seems the workforce as a whole may be in the neutral zone right now. It's not what it was, but it is not yet what it is going to be either, and yes, we are experiencing some chaos.[2]

How do we get through the chaos? Well, we need leaders and good leadership. It is during this chaos that we have the potential to lose our way and end up lost. Maybe we're just hopelessly optimistic, but we believe we'll come out of the chaos and establish the new and that the new will ultimately be better. Of course, we could be wrong, but we're sure that time will let us know one way or the other.

> *Every generation imagines itself to be more intelligent than the one that went before it, and wiser than the one that comes after it.*
>
> **— George Orwell**
>
> *Talking 'bout my generation.*
>
> **— Pete Townsend**

Notes

1.   Gilburg, Deborah On. "Generation X: Stepping Up to the Leadership Plate." *CIO*. CXO Media Inc. a Subsidiary of IDG Enterprise, 31 Jan. 2007. Web. 24 July 2010. http://www.cio.com/article/28475/Generation_X_Stepping_Up_to_the_Leadership_Plate.

2.   Bridges, William. *Managing Transitions: Making the Most of Change*. Reading, MA: Addison-Wesley, 1991. Print.

Section II

What can companies do?

Chapter 11 —————————

Evaluation on Impact

Now that we have a good grasp of our diverse generations, let's explore what all of this means for leadership in the workplace. An organizational leader does not want to end up with the opening statement of his or her annual report sounding like Fed Chairman Ben Bernanke's February 14, 2007, address to senators. Bernanke

> told them the nation hasn't prepared well for the aging of the baby boom generation. Their retirement is one of the biggest demographic changes on the horizon. Bernanke says the resulting demand on entitlement programs could pressure the nation's fiscal situation. More than half a million government workers will be eligible for retirement over the next five years...."[1]

Therein lies the problem. While it is true that the economic downturn has stretched retirement plans for many, it is also true that the loss of employment has forced many into early retirement. Our government and many of our companies have not prepared for this scenario. Our retirement programs, pension plans, and 401(k)s are just beginning the big drain that will start as a trickle and increase steadily until organizations from every industry and every state feel the full financial pressure of this shift. So the demographic change is much bigger than just replacing empty seats vacated by the Boomers. It is also about preparing financially. This will take organizational leaders working collaboratively, especially the CEO, CFO, COO, and Senior Human Resource Executive. This *talent team* must collectively create a plan to keep the organization stable and deal with the long-term implications of the shifting demographics both for talent to run the organization and the financial impact of the Boomer retirement. This plan must be designed, implemented, and constantly monitored and adjusted based on new information. Think of it as a "threat" just as the United States thinks of terrorism as a "threat." The shifting demographics along with every other major "threat" to the organization's long-term health and success must be constantly monitored. When and hopefully before a "threat" reaches a serious level, organizations must carry out plans to deal with the threat. We cannot wait until the threat is imminent. Then, it's too late.

Organizations can do a lot to prepare. Leading organizations place a huge emphasis on getting the right people in the right places at the right time. From a macro level, managing the people side of business is not unlike the supply chain process. It is all about choosing the best quality at the right price and getting it/them in the right place at the right time. This is why we believe that Human Resource executives are equally as important in an organization as Operations executives. They are two sides of the same coin—one creates the systems and the processes for the product or service and the other creates the systems and the processes for the people who produce the products and services. Just like the Operations executive, the Human Resource leader must monitor supply and demand (of the talent) and make appropriate adjustments based on the market, increasing the supply of talent when business is up and decreasing the supply of talent when business is down. This balancing act takes extensive critical-thinking skills, decision-making skills, along with a good dose of intuition.

> **Let us insert a quick disclaimer here.** We want to reiterate that we know, in no uncertain terms, that people are not products or supplies. We also know that companies do not "buy" people. They do, however, purchase or contract for their time and capabilities, so referring to the supply chain process when discussing people is simply an illustration and should by no means be taken as a devaluing of the human complexity and significance.

So one place organizations must start is in evaluating their Human Resource executive capabilities versus the organization's current and future needs. Having the appropriate Human Resource leader(s) in place is critical to the organization's success, especially during radical shifts in the employee demographics as well as the customer base. As with many organizational leaders, a company's Human Resource executive may have come up through the ranks and now sits in the top hot seat for the people side of the organizational coin. This scenario is very beneficial in some aspects, because the Human Resource leader will ideally have a complete grasp on the culture, the leaders, the market, and the organization's needs. And if the leader has been appropriately developed along the way, he or she should do an excellent job at supplying and managing the organization's talent.

However, in many cases, the Human Resource leader has not had adequate development—or any for that matter—and has been expected to "figure it out." These roles are every bit as complicated as those of the Operations executive and should be treated as such by the CEO, president, and the board of directors. Human Resource leaders must be developed to handle today's sophisticated and often legally complex scenarios. If the organization has outgrown the Human Resource executive, it is imperative that the situation be corrected for the organization to be successful. Organizational leaders do not keep ineffective Operations executives, and they should not keep ineffective Human Resource executives either. This doesn't have to mean that the current person loses his or her position, but it could mean that. There are other scenarios:

1. For example, the organization could take advantage of the Boomers' wanting project work or limited-term assignments and bring in a successful semi-retired Human Resource executive to lead the HR Department for a 12-month period while mentoring and developing the current Human Resource leader to come up to today's level of sophistication (assuming he or she has the capabilities necessary).

2. Another scenario is an extensive development plan. The organization could provide the Human Resource executive with a coach and/or a university program designed to develop and increase skill in this area.

3. Or the organization may realize that the Human Resource leader is no longer the right leader for the current and future organizational needs.

One way or another, the organization must tackle the issue and ensure that this position is appropriately vetted and established as a cornerstone before tackling all the other leadership and workforce issues that will be tied to the shifting demographics both inside and outside the organization.

When the right Human Resource executive is in place, he or she will know what to do to manage the supply and demand of the Human Resources side of the organization. In fact, "Savvy managers are right now learning all they can about changing demographics to prepare for radically shifting changes in their organizations' customer and client bases and in their future pools of job applicants. The face of the world is changing and successful organizations and their managers are watching, learning, and making plans." [2]

This preparation is known as the **Human Capital Strategy**. The Human Capital Strategy is directly linked to the vision and strategy of the overall organization and is key to the success or failure of the overall organization. If an organization misses the mark on the people side, it will not be able to stay competitive in today's market regardless of history or brand recognition. Hageman's company Executive Development Associates has a talent management model that illustrates how all other aspects of managing the talent supply chain fall under the Human Capital Strategy.

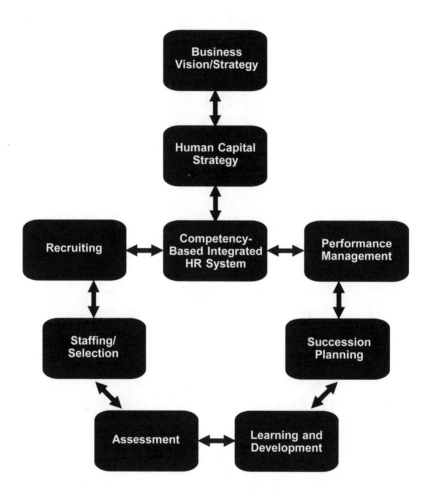

Diagram provided by Executive Development Associates

Notes

1. "'America's Changing Demographics'—Retirement Worries." *Nightly Business Report PBS*. NBR Is Nationally Underwritten by Franklin Templeton Investments, 14 Feb. 2007. Web. 24 July 2010. http://www.pbs.org/nbr/site/onair/transcripts/070214c/.

2. Lieber, Lynn D. "Capitalizing on Demographic Change." *DiversityBusiness.com*. 9 Sept. 2008. Web. 24 July 2010. http://www.diversitybusiness.com/news/diversity.magazine/99200841.asp.

Chapter 12 ———————————

Recruiting

As the HR Department prepares to handle the supply and demand of talent during this demographic and economic shift, recruiting falls on the front end of the human capital supply chain. The basic role of a recruiter is to hire appropriate candidates who can contribute toward the growth of the company. Large companies will have entire departments dedicated to recruiting, while medium and smaller companies may have one or no designated recruiters. When this is the case, recruiting becomes a part of every leader's job. Companies that have a culture of developing talent will often emphasize recruiting as a part of everyone's role, as even individual contributors can recommend and help recruit talent for the organization.

Regardless of who is doing the recruiting, companies will find recruiting has changed along with everything else. Recruiting companies can stand up and testify as they have seen more and more companies move recruiting processes from external to internal in an effort to save money and keep a close watch on the "culture fit" of potential recruits. There is definitely a time when the best strategy is to work with a recruiting firm, but more on that later.

The big issue we see with the shifting demographics when it comes to recruiting is the impact on recruiting high-quality leaders. Remember, the scene in the generational parade is changing, and with the Boomers exiting the workforce, there will be 11 percent fewer Gen Xers to fill the seats. Of those Gen Xers, many are unprepared to step into the vacated positions, and Gen Yers are still too young. It's more than just demographics that cause a challenge: "Events during the past five years have resulted in a sea of change, which has brought a new set of dynamics to senior level executive recruiting. In short, it has become more challenging to recruit senior executives. The aftermath of 9/11, the recession, going to war in Iraq, and the aging of the baby boomer generation have caused individuals to rethink values and priorities in a climate of uncertainty, while the pressures of Sarbanes-Oxley have caused corporate citizens to do the same. It has become increasingly difficult to get people to change positions in which they are comfortable and doing well, particularly if relocation is required. When these factors are put into the context of the demographics, it is clear that the problem of finding the talent to fill key positions, predicted years ago, is coming true."[1]

Organizations are going to have to get creative to meet the shifting workforce needs, and recruiting is no different. They will need to reach out to skilled immigrant talent, recruit from across the globe, tap diversity pools, advance women at a faster pace, and revise a historical age bias when it comes to hiring. No, we're not talking about hiring under-experienced Gen Yers for senior leader positions. We're talking about the *other* age discrimination—*people over 55.* Let's unpack these a little.

Recruit Immigrant Talent

Over the next decade, the changing racial and ethnic makeup in the United States will cause a shift in the labor force. The Asian population in the United States will continue to expand, and the proportion of African Americans is expected to grow slightly as well. By 2012, the proportion of Hispanics in our labor force is projected to grow to about 15 percent of total workers.[2] If you're still not convinced that Mexican and Chinese immigrants—along with those from other countries—matter to organizations, consider this: by the year 2050, people of color will make up significantly more than half the U.S. population.[3] And in addition to immigrants from Asia and Mexico, people from Cuba, Russia, Somalia, India, Vietnam, and other countries across the globe have migrated to America. Immigrants come to the United States for many reasons, and many have held leadership positions in their home countries and are capable and talented leaders. They are often willing to work harder than our native-born recruits.

Tips for Recruiting Immigrant Leaders:

- Make sure they are legal. Even immigrants who held professional and leadership roles in their home countries can be in the United States illegally. It isn't as likely as with manual labor workers, but it is still necessary to make sure every *t* is crossed and every *i* is dotted.

- Evaluate English language proficiency and accent. The person may be a brilliant engineer and program manager from Russia, but if his/her accent is too heavy for most Americans to understand, it will making leading in a U.S. organization extremely difficult for both the immigrant and for his/her colleagues.

- Analyze cultural differences. Immigrants from other countries have different views of leadership, teamwork, conflict, etc. For example, in America, our culture places a high value on directive leadership styles while in Japan there is a higher value on consensus building. It is important that these types of differences are vetted during the recruiting process so that the new leader can effectively assimilate into the organization.

Recruit Global Talent

Another option is to reach out for talent across the globe. Many countries are known for grooming highly intelligent and productive leaders, and limiting the company's search to our borders narrows the playing field considerably. As with all human capital practices, the organization will need to create a global talent acquisition strategy that aligns with the vision and goals of the overall organization. This strategy may include using a number of resources such as recruiting firms, Internet advertising, global Internet job boards, referrals, media, professional associations, university relationships, etc.

Reaching outside of typical recruiting boundaries to acquire leadership talent can offer your organization the significant advantage of an increased understanding of global business opportunities, including international sales and global sourcing of products and services, increased cross-cultural learning, and new ideas for business from the new leader's international perspective.

Tips for Recruiting Global Talent:

- Position your organization to attract international leaders by

  - establishing your reputation for creating positive career paths for all your high-performing leaders;

  - establishing a reputation of excellence in your field through published works, business school case studies, etc., which you can share with potential international candidates.

- Ensure internal recruiters assigned to this work have a global competence in executive recruiting and acquire country-specific knowledge when reaching out to formerly untapped geographies.

- Make sure that security is addressed in the global strategy to ensure that the individuals are both legal and not a terror risk.

- Engage a recruiting firm to assist that has an expertise in global talent acquisition. There are many details to consider in this approach and a firm that specializes in this work will lower your time investment and mitigate the risks.

- Understand that certain applicants and employees have ties to other countries. Foreign-born employees may need to travel farther to visit families—sometimes travel time alone can take four to five full days. Offering flexible time off that enables employees to leave for longer periods can be of tremendous value to foreign-born employees or those whose families live in foreign countries. It is important to remember, however, that giving special incentives or benefits to people based on their country of origin is illegal. Smart organizations will consider the needs of foreign-born employees, yet always treat all employees equally and never discriminate based on country of birth.[4]

Tap Diversity Pools

We've been placing special emphasis on diversity programs for years, and it's time to make them pay off. In a strange and unfortunate twist, new research from George Mason University indicates "...that workplace discrimination actually increases in an economic downturn. A recent study by Eden King, an assistant professor of psychology at the Fairfax, Virginia, college, found that competition for fewer jobs and resources often forces minority groups to the outside. For instance, King and her co-researchers found that when white women and men were told that the economy was going to tank and were then asked to evaluate four equally qualified job candidates, the majority selected the white male candidate. When they were told that the economy would improve, however, they tended to favor the female Hispanic candidate." Smart organizations will use the increased number of high-quality diverse candidates available to acquire great talent and build their leadership "bench strength."[5]

In spite of organizations' reaction to the economy and trying to return to their comfort zone when it comes to choosing white, middle-aged males, the research indicates that "by the year 2050, people of color will make up significantly more than half the U.S. population."[6] It is imperative that leadership ranks shift to reflect the more ethnically diverse nation as well, and tapping the organization's own as well as external diversity talent pools is one way to acquire highly developed and ethnically diverse leaders.

Tips for Recruiting Diverse Leaders:

- Establish the organization both in action and reputation as one that hires and promotes diverse talent.

- Work with Marketing and the HR Department to create a message that accurately reflects the organization in this area.

- Set diversity goals and create a reward system to reinforce both recruiting and internal promotion goals.

- Cascade the message consistently and hold leaders accountable, ensuring that hiring profiles reach the desired supply and delivery goals.

- When recruiting a leader, begin by looking in the organization's diversity programs even if no one has officially put his/her hat in the ring for the position.

- Work with recruiters who specialize in diversity recruiting.

- Tap professional institutions, graduate schools, and universities.

Recruit Women Leaders

According to *The Shriver Report: A Woman's Nation Changes Everything,* for the first time in U.S. history, women are about to become the majority of the nation's paid worker. "Today, women are the primary breadwinners or co-breadwinners in 63.3% of American families."[7] Here is a little excerpt from the report:

> Look around your workplace, and calculate the percentage of women. Now look at top management. How many of those corner offices are occupied by women? For the vast majority of U.S. workplaces, the answer is 20% or less, even though women make up 48% of the total workforce. As *Newsweek* columnist Anna Quindlen writes in The Leadership Lid: "One of the greatest natural resources in America is going underused. And she may

be sitting right at the next desk." Seems that the glass ceiling hasn't budged in years, no matter how many women enter the workforce. An upcoming report from The White House Project, a non-partisan organization set up to promote women in politics, finds that women occupy around 20% of leadership positions in business, journalism, politics and law firms. The rate is much lower in Fortune 500 firms and higher in non-profits (where salaries are typically low). And it's been that way for years."[8]

Women are still a largely untapped resource when it comes to leadership, and though the landscape is changing, it still has a long way to go. Women are not the same as men when it comes to leaders, but that may not be a bad thing. According to a year-long study conducted by Caliper, a Princeton, New Jersey–based management consulting firm, and Aurora, a London-based organization, there are four specific statements that characterize women leaders:

1. Women leaders are more persuasive than their male counterparts.

2. When feeling the sting of rejection, women leaders learn from adversity and carry on with an "I'll show you" attitude.

3. Women leaders demonstrate an inclusive, team-building leadership style of problem solving and decision making.

4. Women leaders are more likely to ignore rules and take risks.[9]

It may be a man's world now, but not for long. Not only is the workplace changing due to age, it is also changing due to gender and ethnicity. As Alice said in *Alice's Adventures in Wonderland*, this "just gets curiouser and curiouser!"[10]

Tips for Recruiting Women Leaders:

- Much like the people in ethnic diversity talent pools, women have often been specially groomed for leadership in women leadership and women mentoring programs within the larger organizations and through university programs. Organizations can tap these pools to find highly qualified talent. Again, don't neglect these talent pools just because a candidate didn't put her hat in the ring: the best catch may be those who were won after a great hunting expedition.

- Get serious about learning and development. Women do not need impressive Return-on-Investment numbers to be convinced that learning and development should be a core value for organizations to be successful. They want to learn themselves, and they want learning and development for others. If the organization does not incorporate learning and development into the culture, it will need to make up the difference in money or flexibility in order to lure highly talented women leaders, because if they have a choice to go with a learning organization versus a non-learning organization, guess which one they'll choose.

- Know that money is typically not the motivating factor for women leaders, although they definitely expect to be paid equally to their male counterparts. Money is something that women want and need, but it does not motivate women the same way it does men. Women expect it like they expect to be able to go to the bathroom when they need to: it is a necessary piece of the workplace scenario. Women are instead motivated by things like a sense of community, security, respect, relationships, and having an impact on others.

- Establish flexible schedules, telecommuting, and a results-based work environment.

- Create a safe work environment and sense of security for your workers.

- Prove it. Be able to point out women leaders in the organization who have been recruited or promoted to leadership positions, receive equal pay to their male counterparts, and were chosen based on their credentials not their looks.

Recruit People Over 55

Okay, now we don't mean to kick any sacred cows here, but we really have to address a workplace bias. People over 55 are often passed over for leadership positions because of their "short runway" (time left in the workplace) or lack of techno savvy. In today's marketplace, the technology piece is central, but it is a learnable skill. Leaders over 55 who desire to stay relevant will have already tackled this objection or will be in the process of tackling it by the time they come to an organization for a potential leadership position. The bigger issue is the "short runway." In the United States, we typically look at people over 55 as being on the downhill slide to retirement, and for some, this is true, but for those who like to work and want to work, they can be key contributors for many years. Think of leaders like Margaret Thatcher, Ted Kennedy, and Alan Greenspan who served effectively well into their 70s. Seasoned leaders such as these can offer true benefits to the workplace, including experience, industry relationships, company loyalty, and strong work ethic to name a few.

There are many people over 55 who are seeking leadership positions and being turned down over and over again in spite of stellar records of achievement and career success. However, there are companies that have already figured this out and are moving strategically to tap the high-quality over-55 talent supply.

In an interview, Dan Smith, Senior Vice President of Human Resources at Borders Group, explained "why the retail giant has its eye on staffing its stores with the older demographic category and the unique approaches and benefits involved in employing a 'silver collar' workforce. With the Boomers nearing retirement age, the pending exodus of the whopping generation that accounts for roughly 80 million workers is predicted to drastically impact the composition and productivity of the American workforce. While most of corporate America is passively bracing for the upcoming shift and sweeping economic impact, Borders has taken a proactive approach to minimize future worker shortage and capitalize on the shifting workforce demographics by driving an initiative to attract and retain workers over the age of 50. With 1,200 retail stores and more than 34,000 employees worldwide, Borders has strategically positioned itself to reap the benefits of employing this demographic to help ring in store sales."[11]

Borders may be onto something. Time will tell, but we believe this strategy will pay off.

Tips for Recruiting People Over 55:

- Create a low-stress environment. Only a few Type As thrive in high-stress environments, and even Type As have usually had enough by age 55. Create an enjoyable work environment that includes

  a. flexible scheduling;

  b. a sense of safety;

  c. a connection to other employees and to the community;

  d. intellectual stimulation.

- Put an emphasis on your benefits and conducive environment. In addition to the more intrinsic needs, this age group also has financial and benefit needs:

  a. They will need to be compensated equally to their peers in like positions.

  b. They need health insurance and financial investment options.

Recruit Gen Y

When it comes to leadership positions, only a few dot.coms are intentionally seeking Gen Yers because they are still young and relatively inexperienced in the world of leadership. Gen Yers may be masterminds in technology, but leadership is an area where natural talent meets learned skills, and great leaders have both. Leaders are not born or made, but honed and forged in the fire. In many cases, Gen Y just isn't ready, but there are always those who are, and the good news about Gen Yers is that there are plenty of them. In fact, the number of young people in the United States without jobs has exploded to 53.4 percent—a post–World War II high, according to the Department of Labor.[12] And they do bring some positive attributes to the workplace, including a lot of energy and enthusiasm, and if the older generations don't bring them down, they can bring some renewed vigor into the workplace. Of course they also bring a massive amount of technology expertise. They are just not afraid in this area, and that can lead an organization into bold new worlds. They also love the team and community aspect of work, and they are good at it. Perhaps they will be the ones to help us all bridge the generational great divide.

Tips for Recruiting Gen Y:

- As a company, have high integrity. Yes, Gen Yers "lift" a little music and hack into computers from time to time, but we're not talking about them right now. We're talking about the companies that recruit them.

- Hold group information meetings.

- Be prepared to engage with their parents. Try to embrace this new trend: parents are heavy influencers for this group.

- Expect interviews to be conversations; the days of a one-way line of Q&A are over. Today's applicants are likely to show up with as many questions about the company and their potential boss and team as the HR Department has for them.

- Try on the fit through an internship. While potential employees are still job hunting, contract with them for one- to three-week internships. Organizations may want to make these internships three or four days a week, leaving them time to continue to interview. If it's the right fit, a little more shopping will only help to cement the deal. This tactic allows both the organization and Gen Yer to "try on" the fit before deciding.

- Provide lots of feedback in the moment or at least before Gen Yers leave the interview. Remember, they are used to real-time (texting, instant messages, Google), so don't let the process drag out. The closer potential employers can get to this the better.

- Design and promote possible career paths. Gen Yers will want to know about the potential for their career at this organization. After all, they don't want to be job hoppers. They prefer to stay with one or two organizations throughout their career—at least that's what they say. They may still be job hoppers, but if the organization has the right environment along with interesting work, they will be all too happy to stay put.

- Before you hire, check out their Facebook page and other avenues to their online reputation. It shouldn't be too difficult in this digital age to get the "unofficial reference" on just about everyone.

In all, recruiting is an exciting puzzle to put together. Looking for just the right pool of candidates and then figuring out how to recruit them is both a challenge and an adventure. Don't be afraid to try some things. If it doesn't work, try something else. Thomas Edison once said the following about trying to invent the light bulb:

> *"I am not discouraged, because every wrong attempt discarded is another step forward."*
>
> — **Thomas Edison**

Recruiting is not unlike inventing in that you may have to do it wrong a few times to figure out what is right. And, like a good inventor, it will be necessary to keep track of each recruiting effort and its rate of success. You'll only know what works if you have a method for tracking success.

Notes

1.   Fuller, Thomas J. "The New Dynamics in Executive Recruiting—Recruitment & Executive Search." *HR Management*. GDS Publishing. Web. 24 July 2010. http://www.hrmreport. com/article/The-New-Dynamics-in-Executive-Recruiting.

2.   "Evolving Demographics in the Workplace." *Personnel(ly) Speaking: Personnel Management Systems, Inc.* (Feb. 2005). Web. http://www.hrpmsi.com/DynamicContent/ Speak0205.htm.

3.   Lieber, Lynn. "Capitalizing on Demographic Change and the Global Workforce." *WPA in the News*. Workplace Answers, 1 June 2009. Web. 24 July 2010. http://www.workplace answers.com/Company/News-Events/WPA-in-the-News/ Capitalizing-on-Demographic-Change—Preparing—(1)/.

4.   Ibid.

5.   McAdams, Sarah. "Diversity Programs Important During Recession." *Diversity Insight*. The Employment Law Post, 19 Apr. 2009. Web. 24 July 2010. http://employmentlaw post.com/ diversity/2009/04/19/diversity-programs-important-during-recession/.

6.   Lieber, Lynn. "Capitalizing on Demographic Change and the Global Workforce." *WPA in the News*. Workplace Answers, 1 June 2009. Web. 24 July 2010. http://www.workplace answers. com/Company/News-Events/WPA-in-the-News/ Capitalizing-on-Demographic-Change—Preparing—(1)/.

7.   Boushey, Heather, and Ann O'Leary. "The Shriver Report: A Study by Maria Shriver and the Center for American Progress on How We Work and Live Today." *The Shriver Report*. Web. 24 July 2010. http://www.awomansnation. com/execSum.php.

8.   Arnst, Cathy. "Women in Leadership: The 20% Rule." *Bloomberg BusinessWeek*. 8 Oct. 2008. Web. 24 July 2010. http://www.businessweek.com/careers/workingparents/blog/ archives/2008/10/women_in_leadership_the_20_rule.html.

9.   Lowen, Linda. "Qualities of Women Leaders." *Women's Issues—All About Women's Issues*. About.com Guide. Web. 24 July 2010. http://womensissues.about.com/od/inthework place/a/ WomenLeaders.htm.

10.   Carroll, Lewis, and Martin Gardner. *The Annotated Alice: Alice's Adventures in Wonderland* and *Through the Looking Glass*, New York: C. N. Potter, 1960. Print.

11.   "The Silver Lining at Borders." *HR Management | The Online Human Resources News Source HR Management | The Online Human Resources News Source | GDS Publishing*. Web. 24 July 2010. http://www.hrmreport.com/article/The-silver-lining-at-Borders/.

12.   Lieber, Lynn. "How to Manage the Four Generations in Today's Workplace." *Workplace Answers: Employment Relations Today: Questions and Answers Column*. 27 Jan. 2010. Web. 24 July 2010. http://www.workplaceanswers.com/News/Changing-Demographics-Will-Require-Changing-the-Wa301.aspx.

Chapter 13 —————————————
Staffing and Selection

If recruiting is getting people into the top of the funnel, then staffing and selection are choosing the right candidates out of the pool and getting them through the funnel and into the leadership pipeline. In the following diagram, the Recruiting Funnel, by Sloane and Associates, Inc., of Brookfield, Wisconsin, we see a good illustration of where we are in the process. The part of the process called staffing and selection is when you have your final three to five qualified candidates. As the organization grows, you can see how beneficial it is to have people or firms dedicated to helping narrow down the pool to the final few qualified candidates.[1]

Once you have completed your outreach (supply), established the right mix of demographically diverse candidates, and narrowed the pool down to three to five qualified leaders for a position, it is time to make your quality selection (purchasing) and put the new hire into his or her position (production). Every part of the process will ideally align with the Human Capital Strategy and, ultimately, the vision and strategy of the overall organization.

When it comes to selecting leaders, there are tools that each organization can tap to greatly assist in the process. The most obvious tool and one that most organizations use is the interview. We are strong believers in the behavioral-based interview and believe that a face-to-face meeting is imperative at this stage of the process. Meeting with the candidate face-to-face provides significant and valuable information about the candidate's non-verbal behavior, presence, interpersonal skills, and how he or she is perceived by others in general. The interview consists of questions related to professional skills as well as personal preferences, choices, and attitude. There is so much more to a good hire than just evaluating technical qualifications. When it comes to demographics, if you're hiring an over 55 leader, you'll want to know that they seem healthy enough to carry out the responsibilities of the position. Just as candidates for the president of the United States have their health evaluated by voters before the election, leaders must also be deemed healthy enough to carry out the duties with excellence. Whether we like it or not, image does matter, and evaluating whether the person carries the personal presence needed for the role is necessary.

Recruiting Funnel

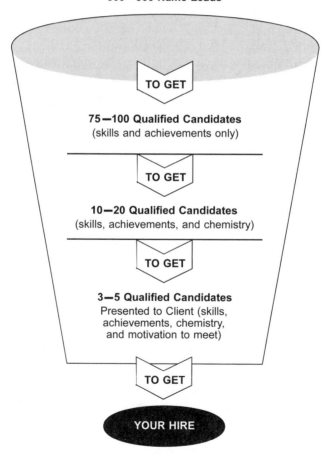

300—500 Name Leads

TO GET

75—100 Qualified Candidates
(skills and achievements only)

TO GET

10—20 Qualified Candidates
(skills, achievements, and chemistry)

TO GET

3—5 Qualified Candidates
Presented to Client (skills,
achievements, chemistry,
and motivation to meet)

TO GET

YOUR HIRE

It is a great time to start evaluating "fit" on both sides. Just remember, if the talent pool includes Gen Y, they may show up at the interview with their parents, so try to keep your jaw off the floor and don't throw them out. Just because it's not the way of the Boomers and the Gen Xers doesn't necessarily make it wrong. They are bringing their trusted "counselors" to the process, and, after all, isn't there a biblical text that says, "In multitude of counselors there is safety"?[2] So, why not? Talk to the parents, too. There is probably a lot to learn there as well.

If the potential candidates interview well, and they should once they make it to this point, it is time to look under the hood. You are making a potentially expensive "purchase," and you'll want to know as much as possible about each candidate regardless of his or her generation. Selection assessment or, at high levels called executive assessment, is a great way to look under the hood. Assessment involves a comprehensive process that is designed to align with the organization's strategy, culture, and development initiatives. The person doing the assessment typically begins with a telephone meeting with key stakeholders to gain an understanding of the position requirements, strategy of the organization, and culture in order to appropriately analyze for fit.

The next step is to meet each potential candidate face-to-face for an in-depth behavioral-based interview, which focuses on education, work history, background, self-perceptions, goals, etc. Standardized tests and personality inventories are also used to provide normative data (see Chapter 14 for more information on assessment).

Once the process is complete, telephone feedback is provided to the hiring executive. This feedback focuses on each candidate's strengths, developmental needs, and potential limitations relative to the position in question. The end result is a written report that focuses on conceptual skills, emotional makeup, motivational factors, interpersonal skills, and leadership style. Here is a diagram from Executive Development Associates' assessment processes:

Position Scope	• Requirements—Culture—Corporate Strategy	Leadership Development Plan provided for the executive
Assess	• Intelligence—Personality—Behavior—Perceptions—Fit	
Report Out and Feedback	• Verbal and Written Report Out and Rating	

On top of selection, the standard processes of background checks, while always important, become crucial if the organization is using some of the out-of-the-box recruiting methods covered in Chapter 12. Legalities and safety measures must be part of the process, especially when reaching out across the globe to find leadership talent or when recruiting immigrants. Doing these steps is just part of looking under the hood. Remember, it's an investment, and you want to know what you are buying. As we mentioned in the last chapter, reference checks are easier than ever, especially for the Gen Yers because their "stuff" is posted all over the Internet. The Boomers and many Gen Xers are a lot less likely to post their "stuff," so you'll need more traditional routes for their reference checks. Just don't miss the "casual" references. "Casual" references are when you call a friend-of-a-friend who knows the candidate or worked with them or knows someone who did. These are often very telling as the references people post on their résumés are obviously going to be good references.

Okay, it's time to make your (purchase) decision and hire your new leader, and regardless of the chosen demographic, the organization needs to be well-prepared to onboard the new leader. What is *onboarding*?

> *Onboarding* or *on-boarding* is a business management term used for the process of handling new employees to obtain the best results from them.[3]

This process can be both formal and informal and will ideally start even before the person's first day.

When we talk about the supply-and-demand process when it comes to people, we don't mean to dehumanize the process. It is simply a macro view of talent. In reality, people are people and not products or services, so it takes a lot more to onboard a new person than it does to onboard a new product. Here are a few tips from Hagemann's Tweets about the process (http://twitter.com/ExecDevAssoc):

- Set clear expectations for the new leader upon arrival about how he or she will be onboarded and expected outcomes.

- Have a formal process so that the new leader feels highly valued and so that the organization is ready for him or her. The formal process will include the typical employee orientation plus three to six months with an assigned mentor. For an executive, the mentor is sometimes a long-term executive administrative assistant. This is a great way to give the new executive culture and history; he or she already has the skill, and the big hurtle will be fitting in.

- Have a set process for gaining standard employee information in a concierge-type way.

- Enroll the new leader in learning and development programs, including helping him or her map out a plan to develop or hone the leadership competencies expected in the organization.

- Have a process in place for the new leader to gain regular feedback and make adjustments.

- Assess the organization's onboarding processes consistently to make sure it is doing what it is supposed to do by creating more engaged and successful leaders. Informal onboarding can include attending department meetings, reviewing attorney briefs on legal cases and the history of the company, attending lunches or dinners with board members, and scheduling time to visit with employees in various departments.

Doing a good job of bringing on a new leader or employee is very important. If this doesn't go well, it can have long-term implications. Up-to-date processes in organizations are now very **employee-centric.** While the Boomers and Gen Xers will be delighted with an employee-centric onboarding process, Gen Yers will be under impressed if it isn't in place, which they are likely to post on Facebook along with the rest of their stuff. So what does employee-centric onboarding look like? Well, it's all about the employee. Companies often spend a lot of time telling employees about who they are and how things "go around here." But employee-centric processes are more integrated, making sure that the new leader learns about the company and that the company learns about the new leader.

Organizations can begin building a profile that will paint a picture of who the new leader is, just like Google, Amazon, and other retailers do for their customers. That way, when a new benefit becomes available, the HR Department can target market to likely "buyers" based on employee profiles—no more shot-gun approach. This is, of course, assuming that your organization has benefits packaged that can be tailored to the individual. If not, start moving that direction right away. If you don't catch up soon, Gen Y will come in and bump you out of your seat in the parade and show the older generations how it's done. The employee orientation, onboarding, and benefits packages of the past are stale and out of touch with the rest of the world: you know, the cafeteria meeting to go over employee benefits, fill out paperwork, etc. Forgetaboutit!

iGoogle is a great example of how employers can satisfy Gen Y and come into the 21st century at the same time. iGoogle (www.google.com/ig) is a personalized Google page that is very customizable. You can add news, photos, and weather and have boxes for your Facebook, sticky notes, quotes, and maps. It's very cool. Even though it is controlled in that you can only choose from what Google makes available, it makes you feel free to do it your way. This is exactly what organizations can do with benefits packages. They can be accessible online, allowing an employee to log in, choose the benefits that appeal to him or her, and create a personalized page to engage and track the employee benefits programs and offerings. Companies could advertise there, make important announcements, etc. In this type of framework, it will be user-friendly impressive for all who come. If all of this can be handled in a very concierge-type way with sufficient hand-holding for those who need it, even better.

Remember, Gen Y especially and the other generations included want flexibility and they want choices. Even with benefits, employees should be able to click on "Add Benefits" and choose from a laundry list of benefits. The organization can put a cap on their benefits so that expenses are fixed or give them a benefit budget and let them choose, but either way, they need choices. Make it easy and user friendly. Make it web-based and flexible. Oh, and make it fun!

Let's talk more about the benefits that organizations may want to make available for this new workplace order. Here is our recommended "gadget" option list for the new employee's personalized benefits page:

- Workplace news and announcements
- Cafeteria menus (updated daily)
- Directions to workplace locations, including an area map and campus map if the organization is a large, multiple-building campus
- Facebook-type social networking but for all company employees (and only company employees) that includes the organization chart and where the person falls on the chart. Remember, transparency is now expected, so for those organizations that squirm at this, it's time to come out of the closet. Include places for posts and chats so that employees can easily exchange information such as who

has what resources, who wants to share resources, etc. Include online work tools for virtual teams such as online meetings, desktop sharing, web conferencing, video conference, net meeting, and web conference. Let's face it: we're going to have more and more virtual teams as we move forward in the technology age, so we may as well prepare.

- You Tube–type employee videos both fun and informative, monitored for inappropriate content for those employees who lack a filter—and we all know a few of those

- Interactive Employee Handbook with a "Chat Live" assistant available to answer questions via chat or telephone. This section may include policies and procedures, legal matters, travel, dress codes with videos, etc.

- Performance management portal for individuals and another one for leaders

- Interactive benefits program:

  - Benefits communication and calculator—shows the employee the true value of his or her benefits salary and benefits package

  - Health insurance—This is the number one most-desired benefit for employees followed by paid time off. However, insurance needs to be adjustable based on the generation. For example, Boomers may need more coverage and be able to stomach a higher deductible while Gen Y may need a lower deductible and more wellness options instead of standard health insurance. Get the benefits companies onboard. Organizations need to unbundle and tailor their offerings to the employees' needs.

  - Short- and long-term disability

  - Life insurance

  - Dental insurance

- Vision insurance
- Flex spending plan
- Retirement and savings
- Time away policies
- Holidays
- Employee assistance program

- Interactive perks menu:
  - Onsite childcare
  - Onsite or pickup cleaners
  - Free food or M&Ms ☺
  - Tuition reimbursement
  - Employee referral program
  - Doctor onsite or house call
  - On-site oil change
  - Car wash
  - Gym information

- Learning and development portal:
  - E-learning
  - Management system if available
  - Onsite classes and workshops
  - Internal and external coach options
  - Career development
    - Individual development plan—integrated with learning
    - Place to house résumé
    - Links to niche areas specific to the individual's line of work
  - External education supported by the organization

- Suggestion box for the HR Department and for the company in general

Okay, that was fun. First company to create the technology in cloud computing format in an easy-to-implement way that is reasonably priced wins!

Before we leave benefits, we think it may be necessary to spend a little more time on a few that particularly matter when thinking about the generational parade. When it comes to **reward and recognition**, we recommend that companies use focus groups from the various constituencies to determine focused reward offerings that have meaning for each group. For example, monetary rewards may do the trick for the Boomers, time off may do it for the Gen Xers, and getting to work in a collaborative team on a real problem that creates new learning and adds value to the company may be a great reward for Gen Y. Whatever it turns out to be, it is important to listen to the employees, learn what matters, and perhaps even have reward and recognition options:

Your reward for meeting the team goal is

a. a day off with pay.

b. a $300 gift certificate.

c. an opportunity to join one of the company's real-problem learning projects with a team from across the company.

In addition to personalizing reward and recognition, organizations should do the same with **work structure.** In general, Gen Y is going to need more structure, Gen X is going to want little or no structure, and the Boomers just want to create structure. Career development has always been considered a perk, but Gen Y will expect it. Yes, they expect a lot, but it will push organizations to be better. They will show up in the interview asking about their career development: don't be offended, just be prepared. We know that most of the changes we are talking about impact everyone but are targeted to Gen Y. It's not because they are more important. It's just that they are a massive generation, they are joining the parade at a rapid pace, and processes and technology inside most companies are way behind the current capabilities.

Employee Assistance Programs can also be tailored to meet generational needs. EAPs have changed to meet the needs of the modern workforce. The shift in employee demographics—such as gender, age, and average length of service—has created the need for increased diversity in EA program delivery and types of services:

> As the large baby boomer population ages, the average employee age is expected to increase as well. Consequently, issues such as child care, retirement planning and balancing the demands of work and personal life have become an increased priority in the workplace.[4]

Finally, we would like to talk about the **work environment**. This too can be tailored. The Boomers may want to put their butts in the office chair, Gen X may want to work from home, and Gen Y may want to come in for project work. Either way, with the technology age, organizations can rethink the work environment. As more and more organizations move to a results-only workplace, they may find that having employees is no longer necessary. If the employer isn't telling them when to do the work, they do not technically have to be an employee. Then the organization can move everyone to a 1099 basis and completely control this part of the overhead based on volume. Combine that with a virtual work environment and voilà: a business that can withstand just about any economy. Of course the 1099s can also work for other companies, but the hiring company can request that they not work for competitors. As long as you are getting the results you are paying for, what difference does it make? We need to ask why we have created a time-based system. We've found that work expands to fit the amount of time we give it. If we say we only work half days, we tend to get the necessary things done in a half day. If we give ourselves seven days a week to do the work, miraculously there is seven days of work available to do. In fact, the work is rarely complete and we often make it expand by giving it more time. If you don't believe me, try to abstain from e-mail except for one hour each day and see if it doesn't reduce the amount of work you have. No Crackberries either. We think there may be many instances where a time-based system is no longer necessary or even best. Of course, we understand that some organizations have shift work and other mandated time frames, so the day of the employee is not over. It's just changing.

Here's what Tammy Erickson had to say about it in her bNet blog:

> The idea of decoupling time [from results] is the rule of the future, whether it will be in that form or not. We need to stop measuring work in hours and start measuring it in terms of task or production. If you look at the history of using time to measure work, it's a relatively recent concept starting around the 1930s, when assembly-line production became too complex to determine what you did or what I did. Prior to that, people were paid according to how many buttons they sewed: by task. In the overall scheme of history, the whole hourly thing has just about served its purpose; I think it will be associated with the industrial economy. It just doesn't make sense to pay by the hour to write a piece of software.[5]

Other environment options that can be tailored to fit an individual include telecommuting, job-sharing, alternative work schedules, and sabbaticals. Any way we slice it, the work environment is going to change along with the parade, and in order to get the best talent in our talent pipelines, we need to be proactive rather than reactive.

Notes

1.	"Recruiting Funnel." *Sloane & Associates*. Web. 01 Aug. 2010. http://sloaneassociates.com/clients.htm.

2.	*Proverbs. Holy Bible King James Version.* Proverbs 24:6. Casscom Media, 2006. Print.

3.	"Onboarding." *Wikipedia, the Free Encyclopedia.* Wikimedia Foundation, Inc. Web. 24 July 2010. http:// en.wikipedia. org/wiki/Onboarding.

4.	"Changing Workplace Demographics." NASA EAP. COPEonline. Web. 24 July 2010. http://ohp.nasa.gov/cope2/ work_demog.html.

5.	Blakely, Lindsay. "The End of Time-Based Management?" *BNET Today*. Web. 24 July 2010. http://www.bnet.com/ 2403-13059_23-237238.html?tag=content;col1.

Chapter 14 ——————————————

Assessment

As we discussed in the previous chapter, standardized tests and assessment inventories are often used to provide normative (typical, expected) data comparison of an incoming candidate or employee for other purposes. Assessment is an excellent tool in the workplace and, for our purposes, can help us level the playing field when it comes to generational differences. Just as a personality assessment ignores the color of one's skin or gender, it also ignores age and helps us relate across all our diversities by looking at personality differences versus more surface differences. Assessment is a demographic equalizer.

Assessments are used inside organizations for a variety of purposes, including

- selection;
- pre-promotion; and
- learning and development programs.

Selection

Assessments are commonly used for selection. Some assessments for selection are designed to measure technical skill while others will measure cognitive capabilities, culture fit, personality factors, behavior, interests, etc. Choosing the right assessment for the purpose is very important. Hagemann says when her organization conducts assessment for selection for their clients, the goal is to understand the person as if we've known them for 10 years and then to provide that information to the client in a way that is easy for them to analyze. When a candidate is appropriately assessed, the assessor can give the employer a wealth of information that will be key to the hiring decision and key to the individual's growth and development once in the new position.

Organizations that implement assessment for selection can gain a long-term benefit as well as a short-term benefit. By assessing all senior leaders within the organization, they can over time create a "bank" of leader profiles and compare these profiles with long-term leader performance in the organization to determine key success factors within this specific organization. Once the key success factors are determined within the organization, incoming candidates can be assessed against this data.

For example, if it is determined that a moderate amount of "dominance" is necessary to be successful in this organization but that a high level of dominance is generally a misfit, then recruiters both internal and external can measure an individual's level of dominance and determine a potential misfit before a hiring mistake is made. There is typically a range set and organizations hire within the range. Most organizations go outside the range from time to time for a candidate whom they want to take a risk with; however, we've found that there is a high failure rate when hiring outside the range for a given organization. For the purpose of this book, we'll call leader "failure" as turning over the position within the first 18 months due to anything other than medical leave or family emergency.

Assessment for selection when it comes to leadership positions is often reserved for the final three to five candidates. Assessment is an investment, so most organizations do the best they can to filter candidates before getting to this phase. Once the final candidates are in the pipeline, assessment for selection is implemented and employers are provided the data for assistance in the decision to hire.

As with all parts of the interview process, a candidate should never be weeded out based on only one piece of the puzzle. Assessment is only one piece and should be considered along with all the other pieces including the interviews, references, résumé, etc. Once the entire puzzle is put together, you should have a very good idea of who the candidate is and what he or she has to offer the organization. Legally, here's the detail:

Under Title VII of the Civil Rights Act of 1964, it is "unlawful for an employer to refuse to hire any individual, or otherwise discriminate against any individual with respect to his. . . employment, because of race, color, religion, sex, or national origin."

With regards to pre-employment testing, Section 703(h) of the Act provides that "notwithstanding any other provision of this subchapter, it shall not be an unlawful practice for an employer. . . to give and to act upon the results of any professionally developed ability test provided that such test. . . is not designed, intended or used to discriminate because of race, color, religion, sex or national origin." Obviously, Title VII does not prohibit employers from the use of intelligence, skills or integrity tests in the workplace. However, the statute is brought into play when: (1) an employer uses tests to *intentionally* discriminate against protected groups or (2) the tests have an adverse impact on minorities *and* are not job-related for the position.[1]

So what does all this mean? Well, basically, we need to make sure that our assessments do not discriminate and we need to make sure that what they measure includes a person's fit for the position. For example, a personality assessment can be used for a leadership position; however, it needs to be mapped to the leadership competencies or specific elements of the job description. For example, if an organization is hiring a leader to be over a high-stress area, one of the necessary components for success is "self-control." Therefore, it would be acceptable to evaluate "self-control" in the assessment because it directly maps to the position requirements.

Again, assessment is the great demographic equalizer because an employer may filter a younger person out because of the stereotype that younger men and women may have less "self-control" than older men and women; however, a valid and reliable assessment can show the employer which is the better candidate in this area regardless of age. And, with the current demographic shifts, making sure that the chosen assessment tools include ability and aptitude for technology (cognitive aptitude) will be increasingly important.

Once an employer has determined that assessment for selection will be a part of the interview process, it is time to determine which assessments are best. Recruiting firms will generally have assessments that they use, and when using a recruiting firm, all the employer needs to do is provide the information so that the recruiter can map their assessment to the position(s). If the organization is doing the work internally or hiring another outside firm to help, there are a few things to consider:

1. Assessors must be qualified. Ensure that the assessors are appropriately credentialed for this work.

2. The assessments must be valid. Do they measure what they are supposed to measure?

3. The assessments must be reliable. Do they measure what they are supposed to measure consistently over time?

Choosing the appropriate assessments can be a challenge because there are literally thousands to choose from. We do, however, have some that are often used, that are reliable and valid, and that we recommend for selection. Here is an overview:

Intelligence Assessments:

- **Wechsler Adult Intelligence Scale—III (WAIS-III).** Based on years of research with the WAIS, this short version has the same reliability and validity as the original. It is an intelligent test used to determine IQ in the areas of verbal and perceptual reasoning. IQ scores are assigned based on how the client's results compare to his or her age group.

- **Thurstone Test of Mental Alertness (Thurstone TMA™).** This is a timed test used to determine the client's ability to think on his or her feet and the rate at which he or she will be able to come up to speed with new information.

The client's results are compared to other professionals in similar positions, resulting in a percentile score.

Professional Ability:

- **Raven's Progressive Matrices.** Raven's is a leading global nonverbal measure of mental ability, helping identify individuals with advanced observation and clear thinking skills who can handle the complexity and ambiguity of the modern workplace.

- **Watson-Glaser II Critical Thinking Appraisal.** The Watson-Glaser Critical Thinking Appraisal is the definitive instrument used by major corporations and consultants to measure critical thinking in high-potential candidates, new managers, future leaders, and all professionals.

- **Advanced Numerical Reasoning Appraisal (ANRA).** The ANRA measures higher-level numerical reasoning skills and is the equivalent of Watson-Glaser "with numbers."

Personality Assessments:

- **The California Psychological Inventory™ (CPI™) Assessment.** The exceptional history, validity, and reliability of the CPI Assessment make it one of the most respected assessments in the world. Its 3 Structural Scales, 20 Folk Scales, and 13 Special Purpose Scales provide a detailed portrait of an individual's professional and personal styles. Built on more than 50 years of research, the CPI™ 434 tool offers rich descriptive commentary for the administrator in such useful areas as interpersonal style, approach to leadership, motivation, and approach to structure and rules, as well as a number of personal characteristics.

- **The CPI 260® Assessment.** The CPI 260 Assessment objectively describes individuals the way others see them. It builds on the exceptional history, validity, and reliability of the California Psychological Inventory (CPI) Assessment, transforming this trusted resource into a leadership development tool for today's organizations. Its 260 items measure more than two dozen scales in such areas as dealing with others, self-management, motivation, thinking style, personal characteristics, and work-related characteristics.

- **The Hogan Leadership Suite.** The Hogan Personality Inventory (HPI) is a measure of normal personality and is used to predict job performance. The HPI is an ideal tool to help you strengthen your employee selection, leadership development, succession planning, and talent management processes. The HPI was the first inventory of normal personality based on the Five-Factor Model and developed specifically for the business community.

Behavior Assessment:

- **The Fundamental Interpersonal Relations Orientation– Behavior (FIRO-B) Assessment.** The FIRO-B Assessment helps people understand their own behavior and that of others in interpersonal situations. For more than 40 years, it has been used around the world to clarify human interactions in both business and personal situations. It explores three basic interpersonal needs (Inclusion, Control, and Affection) along two dimensions (Expressed and Wanted). Requiring only 15 minutes to complete 54 items, the FIRO-B tool quickly sets the stage for self-understanding.

This is certainly not a comprehensive list. It is just a list that we are comfortable promoting based on our extensive experience with assessment tools. There are over 2,700 assessments published, so please just do your homework and work with assessment experts to choose the best tool for your purposes.

Pre-promotion

Pre-promotion assessment is highly recommended and very beneficial for both those who receive the promotion and those who do not if used appropriately. As with selection assessment, the appropriate assessment must be chosen, and it is highly beneficial to use the same tools across the organization both for consistency and for overall alignment as well as for creating a "bank" of leader profiles across the organization. The tools are then mapped to the organization's leadership competencies. The table below is an example of leadership competencies mapped to the two CPI assessments:

Business Acumen	Intellectual Efficiency (Ie)	Conceptual Fluency (Cf)
• Has the knowledge and ability to think critically and make profitable business decisions • Understands organizational vision, strategy, and goals • Understands organizational policies, procedures, and legalities concerning both operations and human resources • Knowledgeable in current and possible future policies, practices, trends, technology, and information affecting his/her business and organization • Understands the marketplace, target market, and customer demographic • Is aware of how strategies and tactics work in the marketplace	Identifies the degree of personal and intellectual efficiency that the individual has attained	Identifies people who deal easily with abstract and complex concepts and who believe in their own talent

Once the assessment is mapped to the leadership competencies, it can be used in conjunction with the interview process, reference check, 360-degree survey feedback, and employee evaluations. Then, the final candidate is chosen and placed in position. Now, here's how this process is beneficial to everyone involved. In a best practice organization, *all* the final candidates will receive feedback from their pre-promotion assessment along with a chance to create a development plan to improve.

For the individual who receives the promotion, we recommend he or she receive three months of coaching based on the results of the pre-promotion assessment immediately following acceptance of the new position. In one organization, we saw turnover for managers reduced from 41 percent down to 10 percent using this process over a two-year time frame. It works! Statistics show that leaders turn over at an average of 40 percent, whether they are front-line supervisors or CEOs, so the Return-on-Investment of this type of pre-promotion assessment and development can be game changing.

Learning and Development Programs

Learning and development will play a vital role in preparing for and thriving throughout the demographic shift, and we will cover this extensively in the next chapter. However, assessments play a vital role in learning and development, and we want to touch on that here before the deep dive in Chapter 15.

The reason assessments play a vital role in learning and development is because they reveal something, and they typically do so in a black-and-white (data analysis) kind of way. Learning and development is typically around "soft" skills such as communication and change management rather than technical skills such as programming capabilities. Therefore, being able to have data to work with provides both the learner and the learning facilitator with a tangible source of information to work with. We can tell you from experience that getting a bunch of engineers to work on their communication skills works a lot better when they have something tangible to work with. Assessments also reveal something about ourselves or others, and that is both interesting and helpful in the learning process. While assessments do not need to be included in every learning and development initiative, we definitely believe they should be included in some of them. In fact, we recommend that your organization choose a base assessment and make that a prerequisite for every other learning and development program. Having a "base" assessment aligns the organization, creating a common language that can be used for learning, performance evaluations, etc. It also prevents your organization from going with the flavor of the month as new people bring in new assessments. For this purpose, we recommend the Golden Personality Type Profiler™ or the Myers-Briggs Type Indicator® (MBTI®) based on our own experience of its effectiveness, ease-of-use, extremely high reliability, and validity. Other tools that we have heard of being used in organizations as a base assessment are The Hogan Personality Inventory and DiSC® inventory. Regardless of which assessment is chosen, all other assessments are used to add additional information and should complement the base assessment. Here is an example of an assessment package that we would recommend to our clients:

- **Base assessment** and prerequisite to all other learning and development:
  - Golden Personality Type Profiler
  - Myers-Briggs Type Indicator (MBTI)
  - Psychological Type Indicator™ (PTI)

- **Communication**
  - DISCStyles™
  - Golden Personality Type Profiler
  - Insight Inventory®, Form B
  - MBTI and Communication application

- **Finance**
  - Business Simulation
  - Advanced Numerical Reasoning Appraisal (ANRA)
  - PREVUE®

- **Operations**
  - Business Simulation
  - PREVUE
  - Raven's Progressive Matrices

- **Team building**
  - Golden Personality Type Profiler
  - Insight Inventory®, Form A
  - MBTI and Teams application

- **Conflict management**
  - Dealing with Conflict Instrument (DCI)
  - The Thomas-Kilmann Conflict Mode Instrument (TKI)
  - Crucial Conversations®

- **Sales and marketing**
  - Business Simulation, BTS
  - Golden Personality Type Profiler
  - MBTI and Selling application
  - PREVUE®

- **Decision making**
  - Watson-Glaser™ II Critical Thinking Appraisal
  - Business Simulation

- **Managing change**
  - Golden Personality Type Profiler
  - MBTI and Change application
  - Business Simulation

- **Career development**
  - Strong Interest Inventory®
  - PREVUE®
  - Work/Life Values Checklist
  - PS Leader™

- **Performance management**
  - Golden Personality Type Profiler
  - Myers-Briggs Type Indicator (MBTI)
  - Strategic Leadership Type Indicator™ (SLTI)
  - 360-Degree Survey
    - Custom to the organization
    - Leadership Effectiveness Survey® (LES), Executive Development Associates
    - Benchmarks® and Skill Scope®
    - PS Leader™
    - The PROFILOR®
    - Voices

Again there are over 2,700 tests and assessments, so this is simply a suggested list based on our experience, and these are just tools to aid the process. The real work begins when the learning begins. Let's dive into learning and development and how it can improve our chances for success during the demographic and economic turbulence.

Note

1.   Schinnerer, Ph.D., John. "Avoiding Legal Issues in Pre-employment Testing." *Crimescreen.com*. Web. 24 July 2010. http://crimescreen.com/newspage.htm.

Chapter 15 ——————
Learning and Development

Of all the potential preparation that organizations can provide, learning and development is the most needed and will produce the most benefits throughout the demographic shifting. This is also an area that has not been sufficiently addressed to date. "Only 46 percent of learning executives report their organizations are doing either a 'good' or 'excellent' job in addressing demographics shifts. Further, just over 40 percent agree that their companies are addressing their overall skill and capability needs over the next three to five years. Perhaps even more concerning is the fact that just over one-quarter of companies has plans in place to address positions that are potentially at risk due to a maturing workforce. Put together, these statistics suggest that many organizations remain unprepared."[1]

The good news is that it's not too late. We can begin with what we have in place and move forward. Learning and development strategies, processes, and programs inside an organization can do a lot to move the generational leadership parade forward in an effective way. Whether an organization has an entire division, one person, or simply uses external consultants and workshops to address learning and development, the impact on the demographic shift will not just happen. The learning processes must include appropriate adjustments in the offerings and members of the talent pools in order to sufficiently address this shift. As we've learned in previous chapters, each generation approaches work from different viewpoints. We can't expect to place Boomers who are just stepping into leadership positions in the same class with Gen X and Gen Y emerging leaders and expect everyone to benefit without creating an environment conducive to cross-generation learning.

Older workers may be dissatisfied working on a project that is continually changing, and younger workers may grow bored if a manager insists that work be completed in a highly procedural or bureaucratic manner that is rule- or process-driven. . ..."[2]

Creating a conducive environment is not only possible, but doing so will strengthen and energize traditional programs. One of the best ways to reorient your development programs is to pull together an advisory group with constituents from each generation. Either choose individuals who have participated in the development program or allow each one an opportunity to experience it personally. Then pull the group together to draft a creative and fun revision to the program. It will be a learning experience in itself, and you will come out with a revised and effective cross-generational program.

There are additional components to implementing successful learning and development efforts for the multigenerational workforces. Let's map out a strategy.

Determining Critical Skills and Capabilities

Critical skills and capabilities are the "competencies" around which organizations build their strategic human resources processes (see model on p. 91). Organizations begin this strategic alignment by identifying the competencies needed to perform successfully in their specific environment and to reach their organization's specific vision and strategy. Once a competency model has been developed and validated, it is used as the foundation for streamlining recruiting, staffing selection, development, succession processes, and performance management. The framework for describing leadership success will also be aligned with the current and future business strategy in order to aid the organization in meeting its financial goals and objectives. So when it comes to preparing for the demographic shift, each organization will want to first identify its unique competencies desired and then consider integrating the Top 5 Competencies Most Lacking in the Next

Generation of Leaders according to the Executive Development Associates and Pearson 2009/2010 biennial Trends in Executive Development Research:[3]

Top 5 Competencies Most Lacking in the Next Generation of Leaders

1. **Strategic thinking**
2. Leading change
3. Ability to create a vision and engage others around it
4. Ability to inspire
5. Understand the total enterprise and how parts work together

---

Across organizations and industries large and small, we find these competencies to be both necessary and lacking in next generation leaders. High Potential and Emerging Leader programs specifically will want to address these competencies as potential gaps in their rising leadership talent pool.

Transferring the Knowledge

To be effective at carrying the organization forward, next-generation leaders will need all their own knowledge and skills as well as the knowledge of the Boomers. Wikipedia's definition of **knowledge management (KM)** is this: "a range of strategies and practices used in an organization to identify, create, represent, distribute, and enable adoption of insights and experiences. Such insights and experiences comprise knowledge, either embodied in individuals or embedded in organizational processes or practice." When we refer to knowledge management inside an organization, we are typically referring to two types of knowledge:

- **Explicit knowledge**: knowledge that an individual uses to do his or her job and is aware of and is capable of explaining to others. An example of explicit knowledge is knowing which manual, code, or process to use in a given scenario and is typically easily transferred to others.

- **Tacit knowledge:** knowledge that an individual uses to do his or her job that is deeper, inherent, complex, and difficult to transfer such as how to work around the internal bureaucracy, put together an effective presentation, or deal effectively with a specific customer.

Organizations lose both explicit and tacit knowledge each time an employee leaves the organization. "Whatever the reasons for the lost knowledge, organizations are slow in reacting to the knowledge loss and protecting their intellectual capital.... To remain competitive, organizations need to examine their knowledge management practices and have the capacity to develop, organize, retain and use their human and knowledge resources. Customers now more than ever want better products and services. As we become part of the global village, many of the products and services that organizations offer have to be transformed to meet these challenges."[4]

When it comes to the generational shift, knowledge management is crucial and "harvesting both the explicit and the tacit knowledge and then transferring it to the next generations' leaders will provide stepping stones for today's organizations to move into the competitive forefront. In our fast-food environment, it is easy to downplay the impact of building on the shoulders of our organizational forefathers. Just as a country cannot throw away all of its history and established systems and processes before the current generation, organizations that try to constantly build the new without learning from and implementing the best of the past will fall short of their ultimate capabilities."

The director of the Institute for Research in Information Systems, Ramesh Sharda, Ph.D. at the Oklahoma State University Spears School of Business, leads a knowledge-harvesting initiative originally designed for the Department of Defense. It is designed to gain both explicit and tacit knowledge. Here is how it works:

- An organization determines that it wants to harvest the knowledge of its employees. For our purposes, we'll choose harvesting the knowledge of the exiting Boomers as an example.

- The information that needs to be retrieved is established.

- Subject matter experts (SMEs) in that specific area are identified.

- A formal interview with the exiting Boomer is set up and videotaped.

- A trained interviewer conducts the interview using predetermined questions.

- Taping typically takes about 1½ hours.

- Once the taping is complete, the interview is reviewed with a SME and a knowledge-harvesting–trained technologist to sort the wheat from the chaff.

- Edits are made and the knowledge is cut and categorized for search protocol.

The end result is sort of like an organizational-specific YouTube on steroids. The knowledge can then be accessed by employees both internal via computer and in the field via PDA.

So, if XYZ Company has an exiting Boomer who had an excellent relationship with a large client, the specifics of this client relationship both explicit and tacit can be harvested and provided to a Gen Xer or Gen Yer who is taking over the account. This detailed and important information along with a proper handoff from the Boomer to the incoming account manager can bridge the gap with an important client and prevent a rocky transition or even loss of the client. In the event of a sudden departure of the Boomer, having the information stored becomes even more important in establishing the new account manager.

For a more organic approach, **Enterprise 2.0**[5] author Andrew McAfee says that knowledge management is creating an organization that knows what it knows. Instead of traditional knowledge management the organization can create a sort of Wikipedia for knowledge management where everyone is allowed to make corrections. It's more about creating a platform that anyone can input at any time with no more pre-defined content.

Accelerate Leadership Development

As we have established throughout this book, a lack of preparation of next-generation leaders as the Boomers exit is one of the top concerns in the shifting demographics. Bottom line: Gen Xers, as a group, are not prepared to take the helm and Gen Y is too young. So, with a Boomer swinging wide the retirement door at a rate of one every 8 seconds, we have to reduce the amount of time it takes to get the next-generation leaders competent and capable of leading today's very complex organizations. In fact, Gen X leaders will need skills that Boomers never needed due to the incredible impact of technology and globalization. There are many ways to do this. Let's talk about a few:

- **Informal mentoring.** This is a process where mentoring in general is promoted throughout the organization and every person is encouraged to mentor others to pass on important knowledge and skills. Leaders are allowed to choose and make requests. There may even be some effort to provide a desired process for choosing an informal mentor. However, the how, what, and when of the mentoring is left up to the mentor and the mentee. Creating a mentoring culture is a winning scenario and can be done over lunch and just during the process of day-to-day work so that little to no investment is required.

- **Formal mentoring programs.** While some investment is required for formal mentoring programs in the form of time and facilitated learning, they can be incredibly beneficial to both mentors and mentees. We often hear mentors say that they get as much out of it as the mentee because they learn about things deep in the organization that they may not otherwise encounter. These programs are designed specifically to meet the goals of the organization. Mentors may be required for high-potential talent pool members, and certain leaders such as VP and above may be required to have at least one mentee. There is often a class to teach the mentors and mentees how to use the relationship effectively, and protocol is established for the number of meetings and the timeframe for the mentoring. There may be some specific goals outlined during the process that are provided back to the mentee's manager as well.

- **Leaders as teachers.** A leaders-as-teachers program is another way to transfer both tacit and explicit knowledge while developing the leadership pipeline and giving emerging leaders access to senior leaders. It has a triple bottom line. The phrase *leaders as teachers* was made popular by Ed Betof in his leadership role at Becton Dickenson where he designed and led the BD University. Here is how it came about:

As part of our blueprint for the future, we concluded that in order to achieve our growth goals and strategies, another key part of the puzzle had to be solved. We'd have to become both a learning and a teaching organization. Shortly after I was asked to lead the effort that subsequently would become BD University, I made the recommendation that our primary delivery strategy for live, face-to-face learning be that of BD leaders and associates teaching other leaders and associates.[6]

Leaders as teachers can be designed in many ways from leaders kicking off programs or offering fireside chats during programs to leaders teaching the entire program.

There is no one specific formula that will work for every organization.

- **External education.** Organizations offer external education for many reasons. Some organizations offer full tuition reimbursement toward an advanced degree as long as the degree pertains to the employee's work. These are typically tied to a contract that the employee will stay with the organization for a designated period of time in exchange for the investment. Other organizations will reimburse specific external classes or even require external development for specific populations. For example, many organizations require their senior high-potential leaders to attend external executive education programs such as Tuck Executive Education at Dartmouth, Penn State Smeal College of Business, Wharton Executive Education at the University of Pennsylvania, Harvard Business School Executive Education, or the many other fine establishments for such education. Even if the organization isn't paying, individuals can attend on their own as long as the organization will give them the time. These programs are designed to create measurable improvements in the individual's knowledge and performance and ultimately impact business outcomes. Top university programs typically offer a range of programs that will enhance the skills of the leader, everything from finance to global expansion.

- **Internal executive education and leadership development programs.** These programs differ from internal executive education in that they are designed specifically to help organizations successfully address their marketplace challenges and accelerate the execution of their business strategy by developing the organization's executives and high potentials in specifically identified areas such as strategy, leadership, diversity, performance management, culture change, fast growth, etc. These may be a one- to two-week annual initiative for the executives and high potentials, an ongoing corporate university, or specific half-day to two-day workshops. The possibilities are many for this type of learning. They are generally instructor- or leader-led and in person and often include external experts as appropriate.

- **Executive coaching.** Executive coaching is a one-on-one growth and development opportunity and produces real business results in a short period of time. We like coaching because it is typically customized to meet the individual's unique development needs and provides feedback that the leader may not have access to otherwise. When done well, coaching is strategically linked to the organization's vision and business strategies and includes interviews and review sessions with the individual's manager to ensure accountability to the organization's vision and organizational strategy. The role of the coach is to help the individual maximize performance, make a shift to the next level of leadership, or overcome potential derailers.

- **Action learning.** This is a process for working on real, current, and important business problems or opportunities, in diverse teams, to both develop the participants and improve the business. These are often used in executive development or high-potential development as they not only stretch the participants to develop new skills but they are typically required to present results and business plans back to senior leadership. Therefore, they gain exposure and access to leaders that they may otherwise rarely encounter. Action learning programs are often facilitated by external professionals or trained internal learning and development professionals, take up between 10 and 25 percent of the leader's time, and span over three to six months.

- **Business simulations.** A great way to both test current capabilities and accelerate the development of high-potential leaders and executives, business simulations are experiential solutions. In definition, a simulation is "an online re-creation of a real business environment for the purposes of learning." In a simulation, the user is usually asked to play a role and makes decisions in the simulation based on that role. The decisions that the user makes determine the outcome of the simulation storyline; multiple outcomes are possible. The simulation storyline is based on real-world business dynamics, and the outcomes of decisions are based on analysis and research of real companies."[7] Simulations can be scenario simulations, board simulations, engage maps, online connected solutions, or our favorite, custom business simulations. An organization that is known around the world for its world-class simulations is BTS Inc. with headquarters in Stockholm, Sweden, and multiple U.S.-based offices as well. What we like about custom business simulations is that they are based on the company, as it is today or with future scenarios. The simulation can be integrated with other learning and development efforts. Participants are forced to make decisions that are risky without risk to the company while they are learning. They work in teams, and the simulation can be used over and over again.

Both action learning and business simulations are great for all the generations, but they are particularly effective at developing Gen Y as they offer Gen Y's perfect learning environment—small groups, operating as a team, and project based. Of course, Gen Y won't like the pressure cooker, but who does?

All of these learning and development opportunities are key both to the individuals and to the organizations who must accelerate the leader development. In many circumstances, senior leaders are engaged and are able to learn emerging leaders' capabilities and how they operate under pressure before they are in an actual engagement that could cost the organization millions of dollars if ineffective.

Notes

1. Lesser, Eric, and Ray Rivera. "Closing the Generational Divide." *IBM Global Business Services: Human Capital Managment*. In Association with ASTD, July 2006. Web. https://www-935.ibm.com/services/ us/gbs/bus/pdf/g510-6323-00_generational_divide.pdf.

2. Lieber, Lynn. "How to Manage the Four Generations in Today's Workplace." *Workplace Answers: Employment Relations Today: Questions—and Answers Column*. 27 Jan. 2010. Web. 24 July 2010. http://www.workplace answers.com/News/Changing-Demographics-Will-Require-Changing-the-Wa301.aspx.

3. Hagemann, Bonnie, and Judy Chartrand, Ph.D. "The 2009/2010 Trends in Executive Development: A Benchmark Report." http://leadershipdevelopmenttrends.com/. Web. 24 July 2010. http://leadershipdevelopmenttrends.com.

4. Teoh Kheng Yau, Joanne, and Suliman Al-Hawamdeh. "The Impact of the Internet on Teaching and Practicing Journalism." *DLPS List of All Collections*. JEP the Journal of Electronic Publishing, Aug. 2001. Web. 01 Aug. 2010. http://quod.lib.umich.edu/cgi/t/text/text-idx?c=jep;view=text; rgn=main;idno=3336451.0007.102.

5. McAfee, Andrew. *Enterprise 2.0: New Collaborative Tools for Your Organization's Toughest Challenges*. Boston: Harvard Business, 2009. Print.

6. Betoff, Edward. "Leaders as Teachers—ASTD Press—ASTD." *ASTD—Training and Development*. Mar. 2004. Web. 24 July 2010. p. 57. http://www.astd.org/content/publications/ ASTDPress/LeadersasTeachers.htm.

7. "Simulation: What Makes It so Effective?" *BTS*. Web. 24 July 2010. p. 2. http://www.bts.com/business_simulations.aspx.

Chapter 16 ———————————————

Succession Planning

Learning and development may do the most to accelerate the next generational leaders, but it is difficult to know where to focus an organization's investment without proper succession planning processes. However, in a joint initiative by IBM and American Society of Training and Development in the summer of 2006, they surveyed 239 learning executives, 83 percent of whom resided in the United States, and found that "...just over one-quarter of companies has plans in place to address positions that are potentially at risk due to a maturing workforce. . .these statistics suggest that many organizations remain unprepared."[1] In a similar study, Achieve Global surveyed "144 respondents with the title of vice president or higher [who] shared their insights on their organization's succession strategy. Results show that the majority (51 percent) currently do not have a succession plan in place for C-suite executives—positions that include chief executive officers, chief financial officers, chief operating officers, etc. This is particularly troubling for American businesses, as 16 percent of respondents also indicate that they have an existing vacancy in their C-suite and another 37 percent indicate that they anticipate a vacancy within the next year."[2]

With the generational parade marching forward and some companies expecting as much as 70 percent of their workforce to exit in the next 10 years, it is time to get serious. "Succession planning is the fastest and cheapest way to get a well-qualified person into an open position."[3] As Peter Drucker said, "**There is no success without a successor,**" and since no one wants to be a failure, the time is now to prepare for the future. And, "as boomers leave their careers, employers can expect fewer qualified candidates to fill open positions. Organizations will be scrambling to move many of their current employees up into the jobs that

Boomers will retire from, thus creating openings in the lower levels of many organizations."[4]

So, what's the problem you ask? Well, we should probably take a few minutes to talk about exactly what succession planning is, and then we'll cover why it is that more companies are not prepared in this area. There are a few elephants in the room that we intend to discuss, so if the idea of succession planning makes you squirm, prepare yourself.

Definition

Succession planning, according to Wikipedia, is "a process for identifying and developing internal personnel with the potential to fill key or critical organizational positions." It ensures the availability of experienced and capable employees who are prepared to assume these roles as they become available.[5] When done well, organizations conduct formal succession planning processes where they

- identify mission-critical positions throughout the organization;

- establish an in-depth understanding of the position from the incumbent;

- locate internal talent that has the "potential" to step in or be developed enough to eventually hold the position;

- gather as much information as possible about each candidate including résumé, annual reviews, 360-degree survey feedback, coaching and mentoring notes, etc.;

- hold talent review sessions—facilitated meetings with the incumbent and his/her peers and key constituents for the position—to discuss the position and potential successors to identify strengths and development areas for each candidate;

- work as a team to prioritize the list of potential candidates in terms of their readiness to fill the position;

- settle on the final list that is turned over to the HR Department where the information is entered into a talent management software for easy access and also given to a talent management professional to begin the process of helping each potential successor move forward in his/her development;

- have each candidate work with his/her boss, a mentor, and a talent management professional to map out an individual development plan with goals, action items, and timelines;

- meet periodically to assist and monitor progress of each potential candidate until the next talent review session.

Ideally, at the next talent review session, each candidate will have progressed. If they were "ready in 3 years" last time and 2 years have passed, they should now be "ready in 1 year" to fill the critical position.

The talent management and HR roles mentioned above can be covered by external experts or other internally assigned professionals who have been trained in the processes.

Seems basic and maybe even a little boring. So why would companies or, more specifically, company leaders neglect (cough... cough...avoid) succession planning? Well, let's just say, it can get a little sticky.

Remember that most of today's leaders are Boomers, so they are the incumbents for these critical positions. They worked hard to become the king of the mountain, and one big issue is that they don't really want to think about someone else becoming the king of the mountain. So this is a big elephant in the room that no one seems to want to talk about. For one, talking about someone else taking their hard-earned position may diminish the Boomers' sense of relevance and for two, *they* are king of the mountain. Do we need to say more? Well, we will anyway. On top of the fact that *they* are king of the mountain, it takes an investment of both time and money to do succession planning well.

When done properly, succession planning is not just something that is done for the C-suite; it is done for every critical position and then planning is cascaded down through the organization as each promotion creates a vacancy below it. This is often called filling the leadership pipeline. It is one of the best ways to ensure that the organization is able to move forward progressively and to make provision for the organization's intellectual property and core knowledge content to stay in the organization and stay current.

In addition to time and money invested, succession planning is an emotional investment for the incumbent. He or she has worked long and hard to be king of the mountain and usually has a long list of scars and medals (plaques) to show for it. When we engage incumbents in succession programs, they often provide very in-depth résumés, job descriptions, etc. It is a part of who they are, and for the Boomers, it may be the biggest part of who they are. It is like preparing for their funeral and has many of the same fears—loss of significance, loss of control, and potential regrets. Remember, Boomers are the ones who set out to change the world, often becoming workaholics in the process. So, the Boomer leader is happy to tell you how he or she made it to the position and how important the position is, but he or she is usually a lot less happy to tell you what you need to do to be ready to "take" the position. It's a threat to who they are. Besides, what if he or she wants to work until the age of 70? Is that going to be a problem? Boomers often say that they have no plans to leave. We are not sure that they have no plans to leave, but they certainly have no plans to "tell" others when they are going to leave. Unlike Gen Y, Boomers hold their cards close to the vest and do not tell what they know just because they were asked or because it can now be posted on Facebook.

We've also found that when we press some reluctant leaders on why they are not establishing a successor for their position, they say they don't care who takes the position when they leave.

Of course their boss or their board are nowhere near when this is being said, but at least they are honest. It certainly would be great if every senior leader understood the importance of succession planning and took accountability for his or her position by making sure all of the appropriate processes were completed and potential successors in development, but as you saw from the statistics, it often isn't done at all. Ultimately the board of directors should be the ones to insist on both a formal succession plan and the appropriate development processes for potential successors. With more and more boards being held responsible when companies get in the hot seat, this is one area where they can easily insist on appropriate processes.

Sheldon Adelson once said, "Why do I need succession planning? I'm very alert, I'm very vibrant. I have no intention to retire," and many Boomers are saying the same thing, but succession planning is about so much more than retirement. It is about preparation, sustainability, and worst-case scenarios. The movie *Gifted Hands* is a true story of world-renowned neurosurgeon Ben Carson, M.D., who performed the first successful procedure to separate a pair of seven-month-old conjoined twins, who were joined at the head. Carson was the lead surgeon of the 70-member surgical team that performed the complex procedure. Before the actual procedure, the team practiced the procedure over and over again. They had duplicate equipment, generators in case the power failed, and every imaginable precaution. They also had worst-case scenario plans in case one of the children died and the other didn't. The plan was meticulous, and it worked. Yes, something could have gone wrong and one or both of the children could have died, but because of their relentless preparation and their expertise, the chance of failure even through a risky transaction was lowered significantly. In this case, a lack of such planning would have certainly ended in the death of one or both of the children. Without the surgery, the children would have never been able to advance along with their peers. In many ways, they would have been stuck, unable to move into a productive and successful life.

If we look at our organizations in a similar light, it is often necessary to take on difficult and even risky business transactions such as a new product or service line, an acquisition, a merger, a divestiture, etc., in order to sustain or grow the company to the next level. During such organizational moves, leaders are often under intense pressure. Sometimes leaders fail, quit, or are moved out when the pressure is intense. Organizations need to be just as prepared to sustain the life of the organization as Dr. Carson and his team were prepared to sustain the life of the children in the now-infamous surgery. Succession planning is about preparation, sustainability, and worst-case scenarios for your organization.

Now if we can convince the Boomers to do the hard work of admitting that they are not always going to be king of the mountain, we must then tackle the Gen X factor—Gen Xers, for the most part, are not prepared, and this is our other elephant in the room.

While the blame can be squarely placed, knowing where to squarely place it is another story. It's definitely the Boomers' fault that Gen Xers are not prepared. The Boomers are playing keep-away from their younger siblings and protecting their own cushy executive seats. But we can also definitely blame Gen X. They have been so busy demanding to take their dogs to work and leaving work as fast as possible that they haven't prepared themselves. And then we can probably also blame the Roaring 90s for just distracting us all with all that money to spend on big ole mortgages, vacation homes, boats, toys, iPhones, and a million other things we really didn't need. After all, who could pay attention to the generational parade when the view in the store windows was so much more attractive? No matter where we want to point the finger, we are where we are and there's no better time to get started preparing for both survival and success.

Notes

1. Lesser, Eric, and Ray Rivera. "Closing the Generational Divide." *IBM Global Business Services: Human Capital Managment*. In Association with ASTD, July 2006. Web. https://www-935.ibm.com/services/ us/gbs/bus/pdf/g510-6323-00_generational_divide.pdf.

2. "Is Lack of Succession Planning Negatively Impacting Your Business?" *Achieve Global*. 18 Nov. 2008. Web. 24 July 2010. http://www.salesandmarketing.com/msg/content_display/ training/e3i2dd2f2ead332946a2c2c74b79091224e.

3. Wheeler, Kevin. "Recruiting and Succession Planning: Three Tips on Getting Involved: Global Learning Resources." *Global Learning Resources, Inc.* 22 Aug. 2003. Web. 24 July 2010. http://www.glresources.com/132.html.

4. Lieber, Lynn. "Capitalizing on Demographic Change and the Global Workforce." *WPA in the News*. Workplace Answers, 1 June 2009. Web. 24 July 2010. http://www.workplace answers.com/Company/News-Events/WPA-in-the-News/ Capitalizing-on-Demographic-Change—Preparing—(1)/.

5. "Succession Planning." *Wikipedia, the Free Encyclopedia*. Web. 24 July 2010. http://en.wikipedia.org/wiki/Succession_ planning.

Chapter 17 —————————
Performance Management

Performance management, the final component of our talent management model, is one of the most difficult aspects of managing the talent supply chain and one of the most crucial to the overall success of the **Human Capital Strategy**. In general, performance management is designed to translate the company's strategy and goals throughout the organization by breaking them down into divisional, departmental, team, and individual goals and objectives. Each person employed by the company should ultimately have specific, measurable, challenging yet realistic goals to be delivered in a given timeframe. When done well, this process creates transparency and accountability throughout the organization and ensures that the overall organization and all of its subsystems are working together toward collective success. It can also become a key innovation vehicle by opening the pathway for manager/employee dialogue. The enhanced communication, collaboration, and transparent nature of performance management will be especially attractive to Gen Y. In fact, they will push us to utilize these systems more thoroughly and effectively than ever before.

Historically, organizations have used a more isolated approach with a basic annual performance evaluation. These were often focused only on the individual, completed only once per year, and seen primarily as another task on the managers' to-do list. As our organizations grew more sophisticated, these annual evaluations were tied to department and then organizational goals. Today, we have very sophisticated electronic systems in place that can align every single employee with the goals and strategies of the overall company. Not all, not even most, organizations have these sophisticated systems, but they are available and will become more and more accessible, even to small companies as the technology moves to a cloud base.

According to Wikipedia, there are also "self-propelled performance management systems" that are an excellent way to get individuals to take responsibility for their own performance. Here are some quotes on the benefits of these self-propelled systems:

1. the fastest known method for career promotion

2. the quickest way for career advancement

3. the surest way for career progress

4. the best ingredient in career path planning

5. the only true and lasting virtue for career success

6. the most neglected part in teachings about management and leadership principles

7. the most complete and sophisticated application of performance management

8. the best integration of human behavior research findings, with the latest management, leadership, and organizational development principles

9. the best automated method for organizational change, development, growth, performance, and profit

10. the quickest way for career building, career development, and moving up on the stepping stones of the corporate career ladder

11. the surest and fastest way for increased motivation, productivity, growth, performance, and profitability for both the individual and the organization

12. the best career builder and career booster for any career

13. inspirational, as it gets people moving, makes them self-starters in utilizing own talents and initiative, automatically like magic[1]

Of course, some companies are not quite to the self-propelled model yet. Many are still below the basics with no performance management at all or just an annual performance evaluation, and yes, some are still using paper documents. Nonetheless, we are collectively moving forward bit by bit. With technology and the excellent systems that are available today, feedback can be consistent, even continuous, and both transparency and accountability can become a way of life for everyone throughout the company. *It can,* but that doesn't mean that *it will* just because your organization has the latest and greatest performance management system.

All of this techno capability is great and can even be done within a reasonable budget, but these sophisticated systems called performance management systems (PMS) are still just tools. A great tool can help a person do better work, but it cannot do the work for the person. These systems are a constant prompt and excellent source of data management for the organization, but performance management is still ultimately about the people. And while we refer to people as the talent supply chain, people are still people not products and, as every manager knows, people issues are messy and riddled with conflict. Therefore, performance management inherently has lots of issues.

As we read in the first part of this book, who is managing who is one source of conflict (Boomers managing Gen X, Gen X managing Gen Y, etc.), but there are many more potential points of conflict such as whether or not someone is getting the results they are supposed to be getting, playing nice with the other kids on the playground, and on and on. So performance management can become conflict management.

Your company can prepare both the managers and employees to effectively implement performance management processes with one important ingredient: **preparation.** Just like we have to prepare for the generational parade to keep marching forward, when it comes to performance management, managers and employees who know what to expect, what to do, and how to do it are much more likely to be successful than those who don't.

Yes, we know. This is not really a new revelation. In fact, it is basic. So why are so few organizations doing the basics and even fewer doing the basics well? When coaching, Hagemann occasionally has a frustrated executive complain about going over basics of communication, building cohesive teams, demonstrating executive presence, emphasizing strategy execution, dealing with conflict, etc. Hagemann tells them just what we are going to tell you now: we can't move to advanced and sophisticated until we have a foundation built on basics. It isn't about learning something new. It's about mastery of the basics. When you master the basics, we'll be happy to move on to an advanced Human Capital class.

> *If people knew how hard I worked to get my mastery, it wouldn't seem so wonderful at all.*
>
> — **Michelangelo**

So the key is preparation, and organizations can prepare in several ways. An initial introduction to how the company handles performance management and the technology can be included during employee orientation. If employees know what to expect, they will know when they are not getting it. This puts the pressure on everyone from the bottom to the top to implement the performance processes, because if the managers don't do it, the employees will know and push the issue from the bottom up. Now Gen X may be happy if the performance management system is ignored and the executive-seat–hoarding Boomers may not care, but Gen Yers—they will care. They want their feedback, and they want it now, and don't forget, they'll be happy to give Boomers and Gen X a little feedback of their own. Luckily for them the processes are evolving, and it is much more interactive than top-down as it was in the past. This leads us back to our earlier discussion of managing Gen Yers—be prepared to receive their feedback. They have had a voice since they were babies, and they don't plan to lose it now that they've entered the workforce.

As a way of preparation, classes can also be offered on an ad hoc basis or required as a prerequisite to other more "advanced" leadership classes. If possible, we recommend establishing a required performance management class for all managers. It will need to include the hard stuff such as how to deal with the difficult performance evaluations, how to document appropriately, how to help an ambitious employee advance his or her career, etc., but it should also include a learning module on the technology. It is hard to effectively use a system that one has not been trained how to use.

As we recommended in Chapter 14, we believe having a "base" assessment that aligns the organization and creates a common language is helpful for both learning and performance management. Our favorites for this purpose is either the Golden Personality Type Profiler or the MBTI assessment. Both are widely used communication preference assessments. They offer a foundation for understanding individual differences and applying that understanding to the ways people think, communicate, and interact with each other. Here is a brief quote on the topic from Hagemann's article "Creating a Successful 'MBTI® Organization'" published in CPP's *TYPEwriter:*[2]

> An "MBTI® organization" is a company that has committed corporate resources to improving communication using the MBTI® assessment tool as a foundation piece. A successful MBTI® organization values and understands the idea that as a company grows and develops, the MBTI® instrument continues to serve a vital purpose as a tool that can help employees throughout their careers. As individual and corporate needs change, the assessment can always provide new and more insightful information for personal development.

So when it comes to performance management discussions, having a tool that everyone can collectively use for communication will reduce the generational barriers and mitigate a lot of potential miscommunications.

In the first part of this book, we covered many ways to help the diverse generations communicate better and manage each other, so for now, let's tackle the more generalized issue of performance feedback while maintaining our focus on the shifting demographics.

It doesn't matter how many strategies, systems, and processes you put into place, they can all have significant weaknesses in the way performance measures are identified, integrated, communicated, and acted upon. It is actually sort of counterintuitive: the thing that managers often dread the most—giving feedback on performance—may actually do more to create job satisfaction than most of the other manager efforts. As long as feedback is given appropriately, even those who need to change or improve performance are grateful for the feedback. The not knowing and the guessing are what lead to dissatisfaction. Most of us have had managers who did not map out clear expectations or give us enough feedback, and we wasted a lot of time and energy trying to figure out what the manager liked or didn't like, what was helpful and what wasn't helpful. We should not have to go deep-sea fishing to get this rather basic information.

Still, there's no way to sugarcoat the fact that it is difficult to be the provider of this basic information. Knowing what to do is at least half the battle, and we'll cover that later. The other half is courage. For that we give you the Lion's Badge of Courage from *The Wizard of Oz,* because truly you already have all you need. You just have to draw it out when you need it, and no matter what your generation, when it comes to giving feedback, you're going to need it.

On the "what to do," remember that performance management is much more than an employee evaluation. It is an organizational process and can provide a significant portion to a company's culture of accountability. Let's break it down into components. Most performance management processes will include

- a company-wide expectation and accountability for managing performance;

- identified roles and responsibilities with the ability to demonstrate how they tie to the overall company vision and strategy;

- written job descriptions;

- expected organizational and/or leadership competencies with weights adjustable for the position in question;

- clearly articulated performance expectations for both the role and the competencies;

- objective performance measures;

- constituent feedback mechanisms such as 360-degree feedback surveys, customer surveys, peer reviews, etc.;

- both long-term and short-term goals with accountability to and results for the company;

- standard performance improvement processes that provide a way for the manager and employee to create a performance improvement contract (this is especially important when performance improvement is required for continued employment);

- user-friendly approach for both the individual and his or her manager.

If the performance management process is on a technology platform, the technology will work best if it

- is "bolted on" to current organizational technology systems, such as your Human Resource information system;

- has a way for both the employee and the manager to engage the system;

- allows employees to track their own progress, report in, ask for a meeting with his/her manager, etc.;

- easily transfers employee performance information from one manager to another;

- captures both the imperative and the useful information in a timely and easy manner;

- has a dashboard so that cumulative metrics can be gathered easily and shared in chart form to senior executives and HR leaders;

- has a high level of interaction, promoting regular communication and feedback.

Employees can help the process be successful by

- making sure that they clearly understand expectations—they should ask until they are totally clear;

- soliciting feedback regularly;

- letting an HR leader know if their manager is not providing adequate, or any, performance feedback.

Performance management processes done well will actually improve employees' strategic, daily decision making by insisting on alignment of personal goals with the organizational goals and strategies—but only if it is done well. When it comes to the formal performance review, we have a few suggested steps:

1. Prepare by thinking through the employee's performance and considering his/her communication style.

2. Mirror your corporate culture and values.

3. Use a performance document that has the performance objectives and measures.

4. Have the employee complete a self-evaluation of the document ahead of time.

5. Begin by reviewing the employee's self-evaluation together.

6. With each objective, listen carefully and then provide your own feedback to either reinforce his/her self-evaluation or provide clear guidance into how his/her performance can improve.

7. Let the employee know what he/she does well, what he/she needs to do more of, less of, or differently.

8. Use role-playing and storytelling as a means of examples and guidance.

9. Be prepared to engage in a crucial conversation when performance improvement is needed—in fact, be prepared either way. You never know what employees are bringing into a performance review.

10. Remember to focus on helping each employee push his/her strengths to the next level and simultaneously make improvements in areas of weakness.

11. Mutually develop an action plan for performance improvement or next level performance.

12. Set step goals and checkpoints for ongoing feedback.

13. Don't run an assembly line. Treat each person as the unique human resource that they are.

14. Don't use yourself as an example of success.

15. Be kind, be clear, and be consistent.

Informal performance feedback can be at any teachable moment and more like a gentle guidance or mentoring than a mandate or correction.

And, don't forget to ask the employee about his/her career aspirations. In this area, consider yourself his/her advocate. You can never really lose by helping another person with his/her career. Remember the employee is not technically "yours." If you're doing a good job, they will stay as long as they can, but eventually most will continue to move throughout his/her career. It is rare today for employees to stay in the same position 20-plus years. Your role as this individual's manager may be short or long. Either way, make it count.

Notes

1. "Performance Management." *Wikipedia, the Free Encyclopedia*. Web. 24 July 2010. http://en.wikipedia.org/wiki/Performance_management.

2. Hagemann, Bonnie. "Creating a Successful MBTI® Organization." *The TYPEwriter* 5:2 (Fall 2002). p. 1. Print.

Chapter 18 ——————————————
Building on Strengths

On October 5, 2006, in an article called "The Battle for Brain-power,"[1] *The Economist* posted the following: "A labor crunch at senior levels is imminent. America's 500 biggest companies will see half their senior managers retire in the next few years." Everyone nods. Many begin to look for the opportunity, including Gen Yers who face as much as 50 percent unemployment as they enter the workforce because it is not the entry-level jobs that the Boomers are leaving. In one of our interviews for this book with a fully employed Gen Yer, we found it interesting that she and her peers consider the labor crunch at senior levels an opportunity for *them*. Her exact words were, "The Baby Boomers are going to retire and I want that big player position." Now, we all knew Gen Yers were optimistic, but we're not sure we all knew they were *that* optimistic. Wake up Gen X! Your competition has stated their position and they're going for the gold. Yes, we know not all Gen Yers want to lead, but what if only 10 percent of them want to lead? That's over 7 million at the most conservative estimates. It may be a little overly optimistic for Gen Y to take on the "big player positions" currently in the business world, but it is not overly optimistic to see them as a big player wherever they are in the workforce, and this is one of their strengths.

According to best-selling author Jim Collins and based on his extensive research,[2] both companies and individuals will be better if they build on strengths versus remedy weaknesses. While we're not opposed to remedying weaknesses and building on strengths, let's take the strength-building concept and apply to the diverse generations. If your organization was going to take just a couple of strengths that each generation possesses and help them push these strengths to the next level, what would they be? We asked ourselves this question and below is what we came up with.

Gen Y

Let's go back to our foundational understanding of who they are. Gen Y is a massive group, even larger than the Boomers. They are entering the workforce as an organized, multitasking, techno-savvy mass that has. They have been pampered, nurtured, and programmed. They are both high-performance and high-maintenance. Here's the high level:

- What are they best at?
  - techno-savvy
  - organized
  - demanding
  - problem solvers

- What gets them going?
  - validation
  - contributing by doing interesting work with a collaborative team and solving important problems
  - their friends
  - flexibility
  - personal growth

How can we use this information to drive revenue? Well, it doesn't look that hard when we break it down like this. We would first try to create an environment where Gen Yers feel valued. To do this, we would listen to their suggestions and implement them when feasible. We would give Google-type benefits as this gives them a sense of the company caring about them as people and valuable assets not just tools. We would also create a Results Only Work Environment or get as close to it as possible depending on necessary shift work, etc.

Next, we would encourage Gen Y to get their friends to apply for open positions. If we hire smart people, chances are they hang around other smart people. With Gen Yers, allowing them to work with their friends is going to go a lot further than trying to prevent it or not paying attention.

We would try to find out what they are most interested in working on and get them into positions to work on those things as soon as possible, realizing that it may be a period of time before the right position opens.

Finally, we would put them in small teams and give them important problems to solve and a structure and timeframe within which to operate. We would give them as many tools as possible with guidance and mentoring as needed. We would allow them creative freedom, and when they bring infeasible solutions, we would gently teach and coach, explaining barriers and problems with the solution and then give it back to them to resolve.

When they resolve important problems (even small ones in the beginning), we would give them ample feedback and pats on the back and, if appropriate and possible, a reward that is meaningful to each one as an individual.

Gen X

Let's go back once again to our foundational understanding of who they are. Gen X is a generation of nomads. Gen Xers move from place to place trying to find their desired lifestyle combined with interesting work that fits. They are marked by and thrive on independence. They are somewhat irreverent, cynical, and indifferent, often refusing to live by corporate or societal rules. They are the most entitled group we have seen in the workplace in recent generations because of their small size and the Roaring 90s, but they are adjusting their attitudes along with everyone else.

However, they love to learn. They are big givers, and they are not afraid to step out and try new things. Remember, they brought us Google, Amazon, Yahoo, and eBay to name a few big brands. And they have also proven to be a lot less lazy than originally thought with more billionaires under 40 than at any other time in history. They apply their entrepreneurial, pragmatic spirit to causes, and they are quickly dispensing with common stereotypes around gender and race. Here's the high level:

- What are they best at?
  - independence
  - entrepreneurialism
  - unafraid to try new things

- What gets them going?
  - professional growth
  - flexibility
  - work-life balance

And how can we use this information to drive revenue? If we were in a large company, we would take a team of Gen Xers who show high potential and put them into an action learning program defined in Chapter 15 to challenge them and have them work on real business problems and create real solutions. Out of action learning teams, we often identify potential new businesses. These are an excellent opportunity to use Gen X strengths. We would then assign a team of Gen Xers to take the potential new business and create it, drawing on their entrepreneurial spirit. We would give them the freedom to build it within a given timeframe and require that they report in on a regular basis so that they don't just disappear for six months without a few reality checks from the seasoned Boomer leaders and some creative pushback from the feisty Gen Yers.

We would create measures of success for the new business and watch Gen X take the business to new levels of success or failure. Of course this would all be done in an incubator-type environment so that the rest of the business was protected from any dot.com, no-profit-needed type business models. We would give them regular feedback and put some pressure on to see how they handle it. After all, we have to know who can handle more intense leadership roles and who is better as a team or an individual contributor.

We would analyze their decisions along the way by asking questions and listening to their logic. We would guide, mentor, and coach, but we would definitely not micromanage this group. Micromanaging Gen X will backfire in a major way, and "Do it because I said so" will never work. Gen Xers have to do it them-selves. Boomers will want to teach them from experience and his-toric precedence, and they can but they have to do it in a way that Gen X will listen. So we would try to create an environment where Gen X would go to others regularly and ask for help and feedback instead of making them feel like it was required. We want them to want it. Maybe the best thing to do would be to tell them they *can't* ask for help from senior leaders. That would probably ensure that they would find ways to do just that.

If Gen X implements a successful new business line, we would allow them the option of staying to run it or creating something new. That way, Gen Xers won't feel slighted by us taking their new baby and handing it over to a seasoned Boomer for safe keeping. Many Gen Xers will not want to stay and run the day-to-day. It's too, well, mundane. But some will, and they need to be given that opportunity, again with mentors and help readily avail-able so that they can be effective and successful. Also, we would reward Gen X with money or vacation or both. Remember they are the ones with the big debts from the Roaring 90s and children who will eventually need to go through college, so money is always a good bet for Gen X rewards.

Boomers

Let's go back one last time to our foundational understanding of who they are. Boomers have always had a strong desire to change the world for the better. They have been at the top of our companies for several years now, and they are now trying to implement their change-the-world ideas. Boomers are a hard-working bunch who sacrificed health and home for their careers.

They also really understand doing what it takes when it's nec-essary, even if it's hard and takes a long time. And they do expect to be rewarded for these long hours and ultimate execution. They want to be paid a lot of money. They want a big title, a big house, a nice car, and of course eternal youth. Well, you can't have every-thing, but Boomers have certainly tried to get everything.

Indulgent, Boomers are indulgent—remember they are the ones who brought in the hippie culture, free flowing with sex, drugs, and rock and roll. Remember, we're not judgin, we're just sayin. So here's the high level:

- What are they best at?
  - idealism
  - applying historic precedent to current situations
  - creating structure and process
  - building on consensus
  - execution

- What gets them going?
  - money
  - materials gain
  - acknowledgment

And, how can we use this information to drive revenue? Well, there's no question that the Boomers are currently at the helm of most major corporations today, so they already are driving revenue, but we can still think of a few ways to build on their strengths. For starters, we would take the idealistic Boomers and have them lead some teams of Gen Xers and Gen Yers to teach them how to work together and to prepare them to move into leadership positions. We would ask the Boomers to mentor each generation and to act as an advocate and a role model to teach them how to get through some of the generational difficulties.

We would ask the Boomers to identify the most serious problems and opportunities that the organization faces and package them into business problems, which we would use as work and stretch assignments for Gen X and Gen Y. We would probably have to do a little bit of curtain-pulling to keep the Boomers out of the actual problem-solving part.

We would also ask the Boomers to analyze the work that Gen X and Gen Y are putting out and provide feedback and poke holes in the solutions in a classroom-type setup for active engagement across the generations. Then we would present these projects with Boomer feedback as case studies to be discussed, just as physicians meet to study and analyze cases to continually increase quality and success ratios.

We would want the Boomers to ensure that processes and structures were in place throughout the organization to ensure performance metrics were set and measured both organization-ally and individually for the employees. As long as they were at it, we would have them create the structure to get the knowledge in their head passed down to the following generations. This one would take time, because we would first have to educate the Boomers on why this needs to happen and insist on transparency and knowledge sharing. Because they want to keep their seats, this is easier said than done, but it is possible. They're not mean. They're just comfortable.

Finally, we would reward Boomers with legacy opportuni-ties—that is to say ways to make sure that their legacy was car-ried for another generation. For example, we may name the action learning program the John Doe Development Institute. There are only so many of these, but we can be creative with other things too like a Wall of Fame or paying for a room at the homeless shelter that has their name on it. The opportunities are endless if we just get creative.

We know you may have great ideas and different ways to build on the generational strengths, too, and we would love to hear them. We invite you to share them on our forum at **www.decadesofdifferences.com**. All of us working together, sharing our experiences, and collaborating on solutions will raise the collective whole and allow us to be successful much easier than trying to do it by ourselves.

Notes

1.   Wooldridge, Adrian. "The Battle for Brainpower." *The Economist*. 5 Oct. 2006. Web. http://www.economist.com.

2.   Collins, James C. *Good to Great: Why Some Companies Make the Leap—and Others Don't*. New York: HarperBusiness, 2001. Print.

Conclusion ———————————————

The 2000s are a unique time in history, from the technology explosion to the Boomer exit, the down economy, and the massive Gen Y entering the workforce. This is not just about a ripple in the workplace because our leaders are leaving. It is much bigger than that. In the economic ocean, this is a tsunami!

It's like we are all leisurely working, playing, and resting near the beach and on the horizon we see something coming—something big. The closer the tsunami gets to the shore, the wider our eyes get, and a million things run through our mind, but the loudest thought of all is RUN! But we can't run from this tidal wave of demographic and economic shifts.

We are all just beginning to figure out what it means, and we can be certain that there are even more massive shifts in the mix. Medicare is draining America's pocket books faster than the current workforce population can replenish it. Gen Yers are going to have to continue to pay for this elderly care benefit, but they are not likely to reap any of the rewards, and the new government healthcare can only add to this deficit.

Our generations must rally together and stop thinking only of ourselves. In a recent interview that John Stossel conducted for ABC's *20/20*, he interviewed a group of wealthy senior citizens about Medicare. They, of course, love Medicare. They paid in for 40 years and now they are reaping the benefits of "free" healthcare, but Stossel pointed out that the average senior citizen is costing three times what they paid into Medicare. There is no way that Medicare can still be available for Gen Y at the current pace. In effect, the elderly are reaping rewards that the younger generations are paying for, and yet the payment plan is unsustainable. As the interview progressed, the wealthy senior citizens did begin to see the problem and ponder what this means for their grandchildren and great grandchildren. This is what we must do now. We must start to see the bigger picture. We must think of our children and grandchildren. We must look up from our own day-to-day living and prepare for the future.

It's a shift in our thinking. Americans are independent by nature. Remember, we are the ones who left our home countries and migrated to America. We are the brave, the adventurous, and the independent. We have the Declaration of Independence, and we all want to be able to live independently. It is a part of who we are. It's in our blood. But this is not the time to exercise our independence. This is the time to work together, as a community—a community of people who cares more about the long-term survival of the community than self-preservation.

In order to thrive as a nation, we have to figure it out. Regardless of how many shifts we have to deal with, it will be helpful if we deal with them as a community, pulling together, helping each other through, lending a helping hand. If war came to American soil, we believe that the American people would rally. Former competitors and political foes would pull together and face the common enemy in order to survive as a people and a nation. That is exactly what we need to do now. The war we face is not missiles and bombs, but economy and demographics. It's math. We have a math problem and we have to solve it.

In the workplace, we have to prepare and make the shifts necessary to ensure that future generations are not left with problems beyond repair. We still have time—not a lot of time, but a little time—to put systems in place, to wake up the workforce, and to prepare for the biggest impact of the workplace shifts and that is the loss of leadership coming as the Boomers march forward in the generational parade.

Since people have made this situation, perhaps we should look to nature for examples of how we can collectively prepare for and defend our workplace stability. In nature, if we look for an excellent example of community, we can search high and low and not find a better example than honeybees. They are a colony. They work together. They are gentle unless they are threatened. But when they are threatened, they are willing to make great sacrifices in order to ensure that the colony stays secure. Let's take a look at how they do it and think about how we can apply their historic success to our situation.

Beehives consist of three types of bees: the Queen (leader), the female worker bees, and the male drones. Each one has a job to do, but the job is never independent of the rest of the hive (workplace). Every worker bee (employee) is born (hired) with her role and tasks clearly defined. Young bees take care of and feed the newborns (new hires). As the newborn emerges, she has a narrow range of tasks within the hive because she is young and inexperienced. But as she ages, gaining both experience and wisdom, she is given increased responsibility. "As they get older, their duties involve work outside of the hive and she performs more and more complex and demanding tasks. Although these various duties usually follow a set pattern and timeline, they sometimes overlap. A worker bee may change occupations sometimes within minutes, if there is an urgent need within the colony for a particular task. They represent teamwork and empowerment at their best!"[1]

Imagine if Gen Yers were more concerned about the health of the workplace than about their own careers? Imagine if the elder generations were feeding the younger generations with the knowledge and wisdom that they will need to survive and create profitable organizations and doing so as fast as the younger generations could receive the information. Imagine if we were all willing to move quickly from one role to another as the workplace required rather than focusing on our own career.

Honeybees also have an extremely clean environment. Not only do they not allow it to get contaminated with dirt, they also do not keep around anything that is dead. The worker bees remove anything dead or diseased and take it as far away from the hive as possible.

We have a lot of still-working but non-producing employees in our workplaces, and the survival of the workplace will require us to move out this dead weight as fast and as far away as possible. In our companies, we also have some dead ideas, divisions, and products. All of these need to be pruned in order for the core to survive at its best.

Bees shift quickly as needed. For example, the young worker bees take care of the brood (babies), but the amount of time they spend on this task depends on how many there are and what other tasks may be necessary and take precedent. Sometimes the brood has to do more on its own quicker. They also share information. They do not locate a field of clover and try to keep that to themselves so that they can be the hero. As soon as they get back to the hive, they lay out the map for the other worker bees to go and get more supply so that other workers can turn it around to meet the needs of the hive and establish a warehouse of provision for future use and reserve. This supply is their profits.

Bees are very much into profitability. They first take care of their overhead by making sure that there is ample supply to meet the basic demand of the hive. This is an ongoing endeavor of maintenance, repair, and supply, but once the supply is established, the bees can move on to what bees are known best for and that is creating a profitable supply of honey. This is their gold/cash. Bees' nature is to create excess honey above and beyond what is required. In fact, the more room you give bees to store excess honey, the more they will make. Alternatively, if you do not give them room to expand, the queen (leader) will take half the hive and go start over somewhere else.

Likewise, if a company is growing fast or under financial or competitor attack, new hires may be required to jump in and do more faster than they would during less strenuous times, but that is just part of operating as a community instead of a bunch of independents. More seasoned workers must also be willing to shift quickly, locate supply, and map out the strategy for others to bring in supply to meet the organization's overhead needs and establish a warehouse of provision for sale and reserves.

Worker bees control the temperature and humidity of the hive. If the temperature isn't kept, the brood will not develop, and the hive's survival will be in danger. There is no way that one bee could maintain the temperature of the hive. It takes a massive, collective, and well-coordinated effort to run this air conditioning and heating system.

This is the same as the culture and climate within an organization. One person cannot maintain the culture. The culture has to be maintained by the collective whole. Employees must first understand what the temperature (culture) is supposed to be, learn how to keep it at that temperature, and then work in unison with the other employees to keep the culture and climate inside the organization just right for both growth and profitability.

Worker bees also send out messages to other worker bees to help them locate the hive when they have gone out to search for provision and supply. They let them know where they belong.

In our organizations, we've often been so independent that we have forgotten to encourage each other and let our fellow employees know that as long as they are productive, they belong here. But make no mistake, unproductive employees will not be tolerated. In a united effort, we will stop focusing on our own careers and start looking around at who needs some encouragement, help, or direction.

Finally, as worker bees mature, they apply their experience and wisdom to expanded areas of responsibility. They always orient themselves to the hive before stepping out and then go out in progressively widening circles, always going out to find what is good for the hive and bringing it back to the hive. This part of their lives is difficult and dangerous, but they do it bravely and protect the hive with their lives. And they work diligently right until the end. Every member contributes his/her own set of skills, giving 100 percent every day for the good of the hive.

Our workplace cannot be a place for the Dilbert's of the world to hide, and it can't be up to leaders to find them. The employees (worker bees) are the ones to expose and push out unproductive employees. Not contributing in a profit-and-loss, supply-and-demand workplace environment just can't be tolerated. Yes, leadership needs to take a stand, but employees also need to have the courage to speak up when fellow workers aren't contributing or are acting selfishly. How can any company be successful at all when employees inside the organization are watching out for themselves, stealing time and ideas from the workplace? People think their small part or lack of small part is insignificant, but it isn't. Each person's contribution or lack of it impacts us all in a butterfly effect type of way.

And then there's the leadership. In a hive, the queen is the leader. Not the potential leader or the lame duck leader or the figure head leader: she is truly the leader. She works as hard or harder than the worker bees. Every basic need that she has is taken care of so that she can focus on her job 100 percent. No one tries to make her into a worker bee or a male drone. She has a job. Her job is to orient/lead the hive. She sets the atmosphere and decides where the hive will be located. She is not lazy or spoiled. She works incredibly hard producing more than her body weight in new larvae each day. She inspects cells and lays eggs. Unlike most organizations where leadership is either revered or hated, the queen bee is encouraged by the worker bees to lay more eggs.

Imagine a workplace where employees encourage the leaders instead of fighting them or demanding that they give them more rights, time off, etc. It's highly unlikely that the queen bee is as lonely as our organizational leaders are because she is tended to and encouraged instead of killed and eaten like many of our political and organizational leaders. Of course we don't speak bee, but we doubt that her every decision is questioned by Gen Y or treated with irreverence by Gen X, we mean young worker bees.

Without a queen in a beehive, the worker bees do not know what to do with themselves. They lose sight of the goal, and productivity wanes. They mope around like they are depressed—totally lost without direction only to become happy again when a new queen is introduced or they grow their own.

In companies, leadership is imperative. Even if we are able to move to more collaborative, results-based models, we still need leaders to establish the vision, create the strategy, and map out the goals so that we can pull together to achieve them. In one of our Gen Y interviews, we discussed the fact that Gen X and Boomers often look to Gen Y when it comes to technology. Our Gen Y interviewee gasped a little and said, "that's frightening!" She went on to tell us that Gen Y doesn't want that. They want to be led and they want to be pushed. That is when they are at their best.

So the **vision** is creating a more united, collaborative, and community-oriented workplace to preserve the welfare of organizations and ultimately our country and to establish a foundation for the success of generations to come.

The **strategy** is to educate Americans on the coming demographic and economic shifts and how they impact the workplace.

The **goal** is to work collectively and share liberally better ways to

- communicate across the diverse generations;
- bridge value differences; and
- ultimately create new, innovative, and viable economic solutions.

Throughout this book, we have endeavored to lay out the shifting demographics in the workplace and the situation it presents along with the many other impacting factors. We have offered solutions to the communication and values gaps and what companies can do to prepare, but our ultimate goal is to wake up America. The economic and demographic war is already here, but we have not rallied the troops and attacked the enemy as one people yet. We are still divided into many factions and parties. We can't win this way. We must be a united people and we must have adequate numbers of prepared leaders, because a community without leadership is lost. We need generals to lead the war. Remember the Top 5 Competencies Most Lacking in Next Generation Leaders:

1. strategic thinking
2. leading change
3. ability to create a vision and engage others around it

4. ability to inspire
5. understand the total enterprise and how parts work together

It's our job to make sure that we bridge this leadership gap before it's too late. America has a situation, and we are giving you a view inside the Situation Room.

While creating a more collaborative and united workplace environment may seem idealistic—even Pollyannaish—but the alternative isn't pretty. Hard times inevitably pull people together or tear them apart. We have a choice. We can successfully address and prepare for the demographic shift or we can fail to prepare for the tsunami on the horizon.

Failure, unfortunately, is easy. Organizations can fail to meet the demographic challenge by

1. doing nothing. If an organization's leaders are so busy with the day to day that they fail to see the storm brewing on the horizon, they will be hard hit when it arrives.

2. failing to educate the diverse generations about each other.

3. failing to provide the diverse generations with tools to bridge their communication and values gaps.

4. neglecting the development of the next generation leader. Development dollars and talent pools need to be adjusted to ensure that the next generation leaders are ready to lead.

5. failing to move out poor performing workers including executive-seat–hoarding Boomers. Listen, if they are making the big bucks and they have the big title and the organization isn't holding them accountable, even the most noble of the Boomers may be tempted to do less and cost more. Just because Boomers are at the top doesn't mean they should stay. If they are not producing, their performance needs to be managed just as emphatically as that of Gen X and Gen Y.

6. failing to see the big picture of how all of this ultimately impacts the success and even survival of our nation as we know it.

Winston Churchill once said "History will be kind to me for I intend to write it." We have an opportunity to make changes and decisions now that will be written down in the history books for generations to come. What are they going to say about us? Did we wake up out of our slumber and band together to fight the economic war and face the demographic shifts with courage? Did we look out for them? Did we make a way?

What will they say?

Note

1. Blackiston, Howland. *Beekeeping for Dummies*. New York: Hungry Minds, 2002. p. 26. Print.

Resources ─────────────────────────

General

Decades of Differences:
www.decadesofdifferences.com

Ken Gronbach's Website:
www.kgcdirect.com

Executive Development Associates Website
www.executivedevelopment.com

EDA on Twitter—Leadership Thought of the Day:
www.twitter.com/ExecDevAssoc

Trends in Executive Development:
www.leadershipdevelopmenttrends.com

Assessments

Advanced Numerical Reasoning Appraisal

- **Description**: The Advanced Numerical Reasoning Appraisal (ANRA) measures higher-level numerical reasoning and is the equivalent of Watson-Glaser "with numbers." Numerical reasoning ability is vital for employees who need to make decisions using financial statements, trends and statistics, sales data, performance metrics, and other information. ANRA can accurately predict a candidate's ability to identify the most important information from a set of data, compare complex quantitative information, and break down information into essential parts.

- **Where to buy:** www.talentlens.com/en/employee-assessments/anra_pricing.php

The California Psychological Inventory™ (CPI™) Assessment

- **Description**: The exceptional history, validity, and reliability of the *California Psychological Inventory* (CPI) assessment make it one of the most respected assessments in the world. Its 3 Structural Scales, 20 Folk Scales, and 13 Special Purpose Scales provide a detailed portrait of an individual's professional and personal styles. Built on more than 50 years of research, the CPI 434 tool offers rich descriptive commentary for the administrator in such useful areas as interpersonal style, approach to leadership, motivation, and approach to structure and rules, as well as a number of personal characteristics.

- **Where to buy:** www.skillsone.com

The CPI 260® Assessment:

- **Description**: The CPI 260 assessment objectively describes individuals the way others see them. It builds on the exceptional history, validity, and reliability of the *California Psychological Inventory* (CPI) assessment, transforming this trusted resource into a leadership development tool for today's organizations. Its 260 items measure more than two dozen scales in such areas as dealing with others, self-management, motivation, thinking style, personal characteristics, and work-related characteristics. Built on more than 50 years of research, the CPI 260 assessment is designed for straightforward, easy administration that respects the time constraints of business. Organizations use this tool in such applications as management training, coaching, organization development, and performance improvement.

- **Where to buy:** www.skillsone.com

Dealing with Conflict:

- Dealing with Conflict is a 15-minute, online or paper assessment that determines how you use five styles to deal with conflict: accommodate, avoid, compromise, compete or collaborate. Dealing with Conflict compares participant's scores to the scores of the general population, and teaches participants to use the optimal conflict style, for each situation. Trainers appreciate this instruments ease-of-use and comprehensive support materials.

- **Where to buy:** www.hrdpress.com/Dealing-with-Confict-Online-Assessment

DiSC® Inventory:

- **Description:** DiSC Classic, Personal Profile System (A plan to understand yourself and others) is the original DiSC Profile survey assessment paper version by Inscape Publishing, formally Carlson Learning Company. DiSC Classic Profile is a behavioral personality assessment. This four quadrant behavioral personality profile test provides an understanding of people through awareness of temperament and behavioral styles. The DiSC Profile is a learning instrument designed to help people realize to what degree they utilize each behavior style bases on their personality and the situation they find themselves in.

- **Where to buy:** www.internalchange.com/disc_classic_2_profile.asp

DISCStyles™:

- DISCStyles is a validated, 10–15 minute, online or paper DISC assessment that produces results in three interpersonal settings (work, home, social). Participants learn their preferred style from three graphs useful for determining strengths and weaknesses, resolving conflict, improving interpersonal communication, uncovering career development opportunities, and improving professional relationships in all life areas.

- **Where to buy:** www.hrdpress.com/DISCO

The Fundamental Interpersonal Relations Orientation–Behavior® (FIRO-B®) Assessment:

- **Description**: The Fundamental Interpersonal Relations Orientation–Behavior (FIRO-B) assessment helps people understand their own behavior and that of others in interpersonal situations. For more than 40 years, this classic 54-item assessment has been used to clarify human interactions in personal and business situations. It explores three basic interpersonal needs: Inclusion, Control, and Affection, along two dimensions: Expressed and Wanted. The FIRO-B assessment can be used as an integral part of team-building initiatives, personal development plans, and communication workshop

- **Where to buy:** www.skillsone.com

The Golden Personality Type Profiler™:

- **Description**: Unlike more simplistic assessments, Golden identifies both a Jungian 4-letter type and a 5th element for stress, as well as provides scores for 18 traits (facets) that help describe the unique personality of each person. Questions relate to five areas:

  - Where you focus your energy (*Extraverting vs Introverting*)
  - How you gather information (*Sensing vs iNtuiting*)
  - How you make decisions (*Thinking vs Feeling*)
  - How you approach life (*organiZing vs Adapting*)
  - How you respond to stress (*Tense vs Calm*)

- **Where to buy**: www.talentlens.com/en/employee-assessments/golden_pricing.php

The Hogan Personality Inventory:

- **Description:** The Hogan Personality Inventory (HPI) is a measure of normal personality and is used to predict job performance. The HPI is an ideal tool to help you strengthen your employee selection, leadership development, succession planning, and talent management processes. The HPI was the first inventory of normal personality based on the Five-Factor Model and developed specifically for the business community.

- **Where to buy**: www.hoganassessments.com

Insight Inventory®:

- The Insight Inventory is a quality psychometric instrument that provides work and personal style profiles on four highly-valid behavioral scales in just 20 minutes. Insight breaks ranks with DISC, MBTI and other personality tests that designate "type" labels. Instead, Insight displays your profile in such a way that you see the extent to which you exercise opposing behavioral patterns. This results in the most accurate understanding of a person's behavioral tendencies.

- **Where to buy:** www.hrdpress.com/Insight-Inventory-Form-B-Understanding-Yourself-Others-5-Pack-IIFB

Myers-Briggs Type Indicator® (MBTI®)

- **Description:** The MBTI assessment is used to develop individuals, teams, and organizations to meet today's challenges in such areas as communication, team building, leadership, and career management. Individuals and organizations, including many Fortune 500 companies, use more than 2 million assessments worldwide each year. Form M of the instrument has 93 items and provides the basic MBTI four-letter type, while Form Q has 144 items and provides not only the four-letter type but also results for 20 facets of that type.

- **Where to buy:** www.skillsone.com

Psychological Type Indicator™:

- The Psychological Type Indicator (PTI) is a carefully crafted online or paper personality measure designed to provide guidance on psychological (Jungian) types using the sixteen types (INTJ, ENTP, etc.) first presented by Carl Jung. The feedback report identifies your primary type and your least used type, and provides comprehensive information to help you understand all 16 types to facilitate better communication and improve working relationships.

- **Where to buy:** www.hrdpress.com/Psychological-Type-Indicator-Online-Assessment-PTIO

PREVUE®:

- Developed by renowned selection test experts, Dr.'s Bartram and Lindley, PREVUE is a one-hour long, online selection assessment anchored by a valid, automated method for creating job specific "ideal profile ranges" on 20 dimensions that include abilities, interests and personality traits. A hiring manager can then use a single summary metric to pick the best candidate, or review report narrative to more fully understand and evaluate each candidate's strengths, weaknesses and working characteristics. Organizations use PREVUE to assist in selection decisions, build teams, plan succession, and match employees with managers.

- **Where to buy:** www.hrdpress.com/Catalog?search-prevue

Raven's Progressive Matrices:

- **Description**: Raven's APM measures high-level observation skills, clear thinking ability, and intellectual capacity. This untimed test is designed to differentiate between people at the high end of intellectual ability. When administered under timed conditions, the APM can also be used to assess intellectual efficiency—quick and accurate high-level intellectual work. The APM score can be used as an indication of a candidate's potential for success in high-level technical, professional, and executive positions that require high levels of clear and accurate thinking, problem identification, holistic situation assessment, and monitoring of tentative solutions for consistency with all available information.

- **Where to buy**: www.pearsonassessments.com/HAIWEB/ Cultures/en-us/Productdetail.htm?Pid=015-4686-786

Strategic Leadership Type Indicator™ **(SLTi):**

- The Strategic Leadership Type Indicator (SLTi) is a 15-minute, online or paper assessment that determines the degree to which a supervisor or manager uses coaching, teaching, relating or delegating styles in correct alignment with the capability and motivation of their direct reports. The SLTI combines proven, contemporary leadership strategies with the breakthrough concept initially com-mercialized by Situational Leadership™ that "one leader-ship strategy does not fit all situations". Each supervisor has to understand the needs and capabilities of each direct report to manage that person optimally.

- **Where to buy:** www.hrdpress.com/SLTI

Strong Interest Inventory®:

- **Description:** For nearly 80 years, the *Strong Interest Inventory* assessment has provided time-tested, research-validated insights to help individuals in their search for a rich, fulfilling career. As one of the most respected and widely used career planning instruments in the world, it has been used extensively in organizations and educational institutions of all sizes.

- **Where to buy:** www.skillsone.com

Thomas-Kilmann Conflict Mode Instrument (TKI)

- **Description:** The 30-item, forced-choice inventory identifies a person's preferred conflict-handling mode, or style, and provides detailed information about how he or she can effectively use all five modes—competing, collaborating, compromising, avoiding, and accommodating. Using the TKI, individuals can learn to move beyond conflict and focus on achieving organizational goals and business objectives. Organizations can apply the TKI to such challenges as change management, team building, leadership development, stress management, negotiation, and communication.

- **Where to buy:** www.skillsone.com

Thurstone Test of Mental Alertness (Thurstone TMA™):

- **Description**: The Thurstone Test of Mental Alertness (TMA) helps measure an individual's ability to learn skills quickly, adjust to new situations, understand complex or subtle relationships, and think flexibly. Developed by renowned psychologists L.L. Thurstone and T.G. Thurstone, the TMA assessment can help support more informed external hiring and internal placement decisions in a wide range of occupations.

- **Where to buy:** HCM_info@vangent.com

Watson-Glaser II Critical Thinking Appraisal®:

- **Description**: The Watson-Glaser series is the gold standard for measuring and developing critical-thinking ability—the foundation of better decision making, problem solving, and career success in the 21st century.

  - Measures thinking, reasoning, and intelligence
  - Predicts judgment, problem solving, creativity, and more
  - Classifies individuals as having low, average, or high critical-thinking ability
  - Questions separate "bright" from "exceptional"

- **Where to buy:** www.talentlens.com/en/watson/ pricing.php

Wechsler Adult Scale of Intelligence®–IV (WAIS®-IV):

- **Description**: In recognition of emerging demographic and clinical trends, the WAIS-IV was developed to provide you with the most advanced measure of cognitive ability and results you can trust when addressing the changing clinical landscape.

- **Where to buy**: www.pearsonassessments.com/HAIWEB/ Cultures/en-us/Productdetail.htm?Pid=015-8980-808

Work/Life Values Checklist:

- **Description**: Identify your clients' most important values in work and life. Help your clients better understand themselves and make more informed decisions about their preferred work environment. This 38-item online tool takes just 15 minutes.

- **Where to buy:** www.skillsone.com

360-Degree Surveys

Benchmarks®

- **Description:** A comprehensive 360-degree assessment tool for experienced managers that measures 16 skills and perspectives critical for success, as well as five possible career derailers. Benchmarks offers an in-depth look at development by assessing skills developed from a multitude of leadership experiences, identifying what lessons may yet to be learned, and helping the executive determine what specific work experiences need to be sought out in order to develop critical skills for success.

- **Where to buy:** www.ccl.org

VOICES®, Lominger

- **Description:** VOICES utilizes Lominger's Leadership Architect® Library as the foundation for assessment. The Library contains 67 Competencies (characteristics generally considered beneficial for career success) and 19 Career Stallers and Stoppers (characteristics generally considered harmful to career success).

- **Where to buy:** www.lominger.com

Leadership Effectiveness Survey® **(LES):**

- **Description:** The Leadership Effectiveness Survey (LES) is a 360-degree multi-rater feedback process that provides experienced professionals with an opportunity to receive feedback on their job performance from the people around them—their manager, peers, subordinates, and customers. There are two surveys to choose from, each measuring 10 areas perceived skills and abilities. Custom 360-degree surveys are also available upon request.

- **Where to buy:** www.executivedevelopment.com

The PROFILOR®

- **Description:** The PROFILOR® is a comprehensive 360-degree feedback tool designed specifically for training and development purposes. It is customized to your organization's development goals and business objectives.

- **Where to buy:** www.personneldecisions.com

Performance Skills™ **(PS) Leader:**

- PS Leader is a research-based, 82-item, online assessment that provides leaders an objective analysis of their leadership effectiveness in 24 crucial competencies. The assessment helps leaders identify development priorities and determine their known and unknown strengths by comparing their own self-perceptions to those of their supervisor, direct reports, and peers.

- **Where to buy:** www.hrdpress.com/PS-Leader-Online-Assessment-PSDL02

SKILLSCOPE®

- **Description:** A straightforward 360-degree feedback tool assesses 15 key job-related skills essential for managerial success. SKILLSCOPE provides insightful feedback on job-related strengths and weaknesses.

- **Where to buy:** www.ccl.org

Other

Business Simulation:

- **Description:** Business Simulation offers experiential learning and performance solutions. Platforms incorporate innovative learning content and cutting-edge methodologies whose efficacy has been proven through successful implementation with leading organizations around the world. Simulation tools allow companies to develop the skills and capabilities within all levels of their organization, and these competencies ultimately drive improved business results.

- **Where to buy:** www.bts.com

Crucial Conversations® Book and Workshops:

- **Description:** Get unstuck with best practice skills for high-stakes interactions. Whenever you're not getting the results you're looking for, it's likely that a crucial conversation is keeping you stuck. Whether it's a problem with poor quality, slow time-to-market, declining customer satisfaction, or a strained relationship, if you can't talk honestly with nearly anybody about almost anything, you can expect poor results. Make crucial conversations skills your best practices and everything gets better.

- **Where to buy:** www.vitalsmarts.com/crucial conversationstraining.aspx

The Recruiting Funnel:

- **Description**: Study and learn your objectives, develop your candidate profile, understand your hiring process, and discover the main selling points of your opportunity.

- **Where to buy:** www.sloaneassociates.com/

Tuck Executive Education at Dartmouth:

- **Website:** www.tuck.dartmouth.edu/exec

Penn State Smeal College of Business:

- **Website:** www.smeal.psu.edu

Wharton Executive Education at the University of Pennsylvania:

- **Website:** www.executiveeducation.wharton.upenn.edu/

Harvard Business School Executive Education:

- **Website:** www.exed.hbs.edu/Pages/default.aspx